T0195570

Soha Bechara

RESISTANCE

My Life for Lebanon

**English Translation by
Gabriel Levine**

**With a Preface by
Sondra Hale**

Soft Skull Press

*To my parents,
to the imprisoned and defiant.*

Resistance: My Life for Lebanon
©2003 Soha Bechara
translation ©2003 Gabriel Levine

Book Design: David Janik

Soft Skull Press
New York, NY
www.softskull.com

Library of Congress Cataloging-in-Publication Data

Béchara, Souha.
  [Résistante. English]
  Resistance : my life for Lebanon / by Soha Bechara ; English
translation by Gabriel Levine.
      p. cm.
  ISBN 1-887128-80-8 (pbk.)
  1. Arab-Israeli conflict–Personal narratives. 2. Political
prisoners–Lebanon. 3. Lebanon–History–Israeli intervention,
1982-1984–Personal narratives. I. Title: My life for Lebanon. II.
Title.
DS119.76 .B4313 2003
956.9204'4'092–dc21

                                              2003013839

Cet ouvrage, publié dans le cadre d'un programme d'aide à la publication,
bénéficie du soutien du Ministère des Affaires étrangères et du Service
Culturel de l'Ambassade de France aux Etats-Unis.

This work, published as part of a program of aid for publication, received
support from the French Ministry of Foreign Affais and the Cultural
Services of the French Embassy in the United States.

ISBN: 978-1-88712-880-3

Printed in the United States of America

To the martyrs.

To remember.

PREFACE

Sondra Hale, Professor of
Anthropology and Women's Studies
University of California, Los Angeles

This is a rare document. Our libraries still exhibit a dearth of personal narratives by young women who have done extraordinary things. Older women, yes, famous women, indeed. But the gift of a personal narrative—as memoir—by an "ordinary" young woman (no human is ordinary) is rare, and even rarer when that woman is an Arab. Souha Bechara—young, Lebanese, Christian, communist, resistance fighter, attempted assassin, prisoner, torture survivor, hero to many.

This document is not only rare as a personal testimony by an Arab woman political figure, but it is uncommon for women to write prison memoirs, a respected genre and outlet for political men (Antonio Gramsci comes to mind). Prison is an experience most women prisoners have wanted to bury.

Unusual though this memoir may be, it is also part of a growing literature on international women's movements and women's participation in revolutions, collective actions, strikes, civil disobedience, armed resistance, grassroots organizing, violent acts of sabotage and terrorism, counter-hegemonic operations, liberation movements, and wars.

One interpretation is that in many of these above activities women have been carrying out operations designed by men and led by men. It is argued that women have seldom been part of the planning or leadership and are oftentimes indoctrinated by male cadre or hoodwinked by the political culture into which they are born. The unreconstructed feminist literature on Algeria's liberation war is an example.

Another interpretation of women's activism in gender-integrated activism is that women are free agents, engaging in self-empowering endeavors of their own making and fully conscious of the meanings and ramifications of their acts. This is clearly a rejection of the "false consciousness" approach.

Souha Bechara, seemingly cognizant of the possibility that the reader might question her developed consciousness or agency, is keen to present her "operation" as carried out completely of her own free will. In the epilogue she asserts, "I accepted the idea of dying for my country." And, as almost a final justification for joining the resistance and a denial that she was indoctrinated, she exclaims, "[M]y own blood began to beat in rhythm with the blood around me." In this way she sees herself as an organic militant.

Bechara chose dramatic, yet simple and chilling, ways to set the stage. The first line of the memoir is: "Cell Number 7, for solitary confinement." As for Antoine Lahad, a name introduced in the early pages, she remarks, without irony, "Our paths had crossed once before, twelve years earlier."

Souha Bechara, a university student and militant against Israeli occupation of South Lebanon, was sent by male cadre of the Lebanese Communist Party (LCP) in 1988 to assassinate Antoine Lahad, a general in the South Lebanese Army (SLA), a pro-Israeli, predominantly Christian militia that controlled the South as a proxy for Israel. The attempt failed and Bechara was arrested, tortured, and imprisoned for ten years in Khiam prison in South Lebanon.

The memoir begins in sweet tones, portraying her village life in Deir Mimas in South Lebanon. Although she moves simply through her nearly idyllic depiction of life before the 1982 Israeli invasion and occupation ("Life was simple like this"), the gentle, evocative prose is ruptured dramatically at points in the narrative. For example, Bechara refers to the wedding of her cousins that involved nearly the whole village in food, drink, and merriment. The festivities went on for seven days and seven nights and everyone was very happy. Then she sobers us with one of those ruptures: "They were married in 1976. It remains in our collective memory as the last great village wedding, belonging to that golden age broken by the war, the war which would first divide and then scatter us."

Despite the occasional dramatic markers that jolt one, this memoir is a skillful weaving together of the personal, historical, and political. It is a seamless account of a crucial time in Lebanon's contemporary history. Personalizing the story only underscores the high drama of what was to be one of the most fractious, controversial, and complicated conflicts of our time.

Bechara builds the tension through the prologue and the first three chapters. She is eager to weave into her narrative memories of the ingredients in her early life that were to sustain her through her ordeal, for example, her moral and ethical upbringing in which she was told by her mother, "[A]bove all one must never denounce another." Imagine the impact of such teachings to a torture victim who never relented! Imagine the steadfastness she learned from her father's commitment to communism in the face of constant danger and persecution! Family love and closeness also generated in Bechara a self-confidence that prevailed under the harsh conditions of prison life, making her more resilient than most of the other incarcerated women.

One may have wondered about Bechara's stress on her athleticism, which seemed almost frivolous in the face of earth-shaking political events. Yet her early abilities and interest in sports and fitness, uncommon for South Lebanese women, later proved invaluable in two ways: they led to the aerobics instructor job that was to place Bechara inside General Lahad's house, and the fitness helped her physically endure the torture and inhuman prison conditions.

Not only does Bechara make the reader privy to the above moral teachings of her parents in the war years, but privy to the practical, "street" socialization that was necessary for survival. The socialization process had to change. How innocence must have drained from children! Amidst a childhood spent not being able to touch toys found in the streets or open fields for fear of booby-traps, nor even lean on a parked car, Bechara demonstrates the development of her political consciousness.

She describes how, after 1975, she saw her culture and history disappearing, taking with it her childhood. She recounts how the daily lives of most Lebanese were "marked by unnatural alliances, internal divisions, and shifting fronts." The toll that the civil war took on Lebanese personal lives, turning nearly everything upside down, cannot be over-dramatized. Trying to escape violence and war when violence and war shifted as well, Bechara's family moved back and forth from South Lebanon to Beirut, as did many people, only to see Beirut become a center of the war. Although Beirut did not serve as an escape from the war, Bechara made the most of the situation. Beirut became the site of her concrete contacts with the leftist/nationalist resistance movement and, ultimately, the place where she received political education and some training.

Bechara remembers that the war often took on a life of its own, having shed the initiating ideologies and agendas. Despite international coverage that mostly presented the conflict as Christian versus Muslim or left versus right, or Palestinian versus everyone else, the war was one of the most fluid, shifting, and complex we have ever seen. Militaries and militias were all politicized and military leaders often lost sight of the very civilians they were sworn (and paid) to protect.

In the midst of all the upheavals Bechara was a steadfast nationalist. Her identity statement, clear and simple, appears in the fourth chapter, "Politics": "I was not a Lebanese Christian—I was first of all Lebanese, and then from a Greek Orthodox family." She skillfully develops this consciousness for the reader, tying her progression toward communism and nationalism to some of the capstone events of the war and occupations. Simultaneously, Bechara not only argues for the necessity (almost inevitability) of the formation of the United Lebanese resistance in June 1982, but presages her own activism in the movement.

Bechara's activism in the Union of Young Democrats, which was associated with the Lebanese Communist Party (LCP), was her official window into the conflict. She undertook tradition-al gender-bound jobs at first—medical-support/nurturing, cooking, cleaning. It was another example of women serving as military irregulars, until very recently a common role for women in the military histories of most societies. However, because of Bechara's education (she was by then a university student of science), she began to work in intelligence-gathering, shuttling back and forth from Beirut to South Lebanon. The intelligence she gathered was used to set up the "operation," the assassination of General Lahad. Upon her insistence, that assignment was given to her.

Chapter 8 ("The Operation," a euphemism for the assassination attempt) is suspenseful. The next chapter, "The Arrest," is chilling and frightening. And chapter 10 ("Khiam," the name of the most notorious, now closed, prison in Lebanon, which was located in the South and controlled by the Israelis through their proxy, the SLA) is a portrait of fear, isolation, torture, and humiliation.

The remainder of the memoir is mainly about survival in Khiam prison, but it is also about female bonding, the possibility of leaps across ideologies and religions, as the development of Bechara's friendship with a Hezbollah activist demonstrates. "[Hanan and I] shared the same vision: a resistance movement in which each could find his or her own place, fighting against an occupying army." The last chapters of the memoir are, as well, a story of the transcendence of the human spirit.

The prison years are a story of ingenious technology: for example, pulling a nail from a shoe and crafting a needle from it, using olive pits to make prayerbeads, and creating board games from scraps. Both the invention of math games and eventually the writing of poetry were important in keeping Bechara's mind sharp, staving off boredom, and recording both the misery and beauty around her. Eventually she began to keep a prison journal.

As the years in prison passed, it could not have been easy for Bechara to see so many prisoners released before her. Finally, on September 3, 1998, after an international campaign, she was released.

What was Bechara left with? What had been gained? Where did her sacrifices and acts leave other women? Was she to become a role model? What did her exposure of Khiam prison conditions do for other prisoners in some of the Middle East's most notorious prisons? Did her "operation" change the face of the civil war? Perhaps, most importantly, because this is a memoir, where did the experience leave Bechara? How was she changed?

What can we make of Bechara's relationship to the LCP? She refers to herself as a "fellow traveler" and expresses a great deal of ambivalence toward the Communist Party. She was attracted, as many of us of my generation have been, to the romance of communism and revolution. In her case, she was attracted to the LCP's defense of "nationhood," the cause of a unified Lebanon. She claims, frankly, "I had become involved with the Lebanese Communist Party for reasons that had nothing to do with Marxist theory." However, because she is aware some readers might be tempted to accuse Bechara's male LCP handlers of using her, she is careful to shield them. Nonetheless, in chapter 6, "Commitment," one begins to develop a picture of men in the movement manipulating women. Bechara, herself, however, attempts to subvert such thinking. About her handler, Rabih, she says, seemingly ingenuously, "He had sent me into the lion's den," quickly noting it was "the place where I had burned to go." Then, "[H]e had wondered about the fate of his young insurgent . . . ."

In the epilogue, Bechara sums up her politics. For the Lebanese civil war itself she had little tolerance: the various Lebanese factions, plus the Palestinians "had torn each other to shreds, and after a peace which refused to deal with the damage they had done each other, they remained deeply divided . . . ." A nationalist to the end, she refers to the civil war struggle as "a vain illusion" and compares it unfavorably with the resistance struggle against Israel.

Perhaps Bechara cannot, just five years out of prison, allow herself to enter into the feminist or any critique of nationalism. What would a unified Lebanon free of Israel, Syria (virtually unmentioned), and Palestinians mean for Lebanese women? For the Lebanese working class and peasantry?

Bechara, despite grim memories of conflict and horror, ends on a high-spirited note. She is full of humanism and hope. This is a memoir devoid of bitterness, except toward the fratricide we have known as Lebanon. Still, she leaves us wondering how long she will feel she is waking up in prison and if her memoir would have had a different tone and politics had she succeeded in killing Antoine Lahad.

PROLOGUE

Cell number 7, solitary confinement. In my memory, it was not so small.

Now, standing before it, I am slow to understand. I lived there, cramped between those walls. I spent ten years of my life in that prison, a third of my days, a third of my nights.

I am back in Khiam, in southern Lebanon. A crowd presses around me. The dreaded prison, the agonizing symbol of the dark years of Israeli occupation, has become a site of pilgrimage. The mob of visitors mills about incredulously. They are moved, imagining the pain and suffering endured in that place. They wander through the rooms for interrogation and torture, the infamous dungeons through which so many men and women have already passed.

A week earlier, history had burst into the present. On May 22, 2000, Israel hastily pulled out of the zone in southern Lebanon it had occupied since 1978. In the weeks before the Israeli retreat, the Lebanese proxy militias had understood that they were running out of options, and that they would soon be left to fend for themselves. They began to lay down their arms and surrender to Hezbollah, now the spearhead of Lebanese resistance to the occupation. For the Israeli Army, losing the protection of the militias meant that the moment had come to cut their losses and get out. In less than 48 hours they abandoned their positions, dynamited their fortifications, and pulled back with no casualties to the other side of the border.

On their way, they might have noticed a man who had come to take stock of the disaster. He had returned too late from a trip to France, where he had brought his family to live. He was powerless to check the tide of events. It was Antoine Lahad, the head of the Israeli-supported Lebanese auxiliaries, general of a dead army. He stood and cursed his former protectors for their treachery, cursed them for abandoning hundreds of men in the field—men who had fought, and often died, for a country not their own.

Our paths had crossed once before, twelve years earlier.

I was a communist student from a Greek Orthodox family, but above all I was Lebanese. Still a teenager, I had gone to fight against everything he stood for, against the foreign presence on my land. I paid for it with my freedom. I was thrown into a cell, without trial, and without knowing for how long.

Ten years of my life.

I have not spent a single day since I was freed without thinking of the camp, of those men and women who suffered there. My time in Khiam continues to haunt me, sometimes taking me by surprise. One morning in Paris, my temporary home, I received a package from Lebanon. Inside was a little cushion. I took it out of its box and put it on my desk, thinking no more about it. It looked like a simple present. Later in the day, I understood. I undid the seam of the cushion and took from inside the tiny scraps of paper scrawled with a handwriting that I immediately recognized.

It was my own. Tears of emotion welled up in my eyes. I spread the treasures out on my bed. Once again, I was there, with the smells, sights, and sounds of Khiam.

A part of me still locked up there had been released, rescued by a fellow prisoner when she was freed. They were my prison poems, written in secret. I had been unable to take them with me when the gates were abruptly opened.

That memory could still be in chains. Today, this book fulfills those words.

1 DEIR MIMAS

One day, I will return to Deir Mimas.

Deir Mimas, in southern Lebanon, was our village—a simple village of a hundred terrace-roofed homes and five churches, built into a hillside and surrounded by olive groves. Our house was off to the side, high up on the hill, but if you took a short tumble down the slope you'd find yourself right in a church steeple's shadow. My grandfather Hanna had built it himself. A cube of concrete and light-colored stones set with windows and doors, it was planted in the midst of leafy gardens and encircled by pomegranate trees. Standing nearby was a tall fig tree that bore fruit all year long. In that house of three rooms and a veranda, my grandparents had raised five children, including my father. The family home of my mother's parents was just nearby.

I spent my childhood holidays there, in that village.

I played, running with my cousins through the narrow streets. I helped my mother in the fields. I swam in the river down in the valley. I climbed to the top of the hill where, on the next ridge, I could see the Beaufort Castle, built by the Crusaders on the road to Jerusalem and held in those days by the Lebanese Army.

It was on one of these walks that I first visited Khiam, only a few miles from our village. It was a military camp like any other, an old garrison from the colonial days, a barracks perched high up among the oaks that towered above its surroundings. The market town of Khiam, the largest in the region, lay spread out at the foot of the camp. I remember some young soldiers on guard duty with whom we exchanged a few words. It wasn't a very memorable scene. I could never have imagined what that fortress would come to mean to me fifteen years later.

And so passed my childhood summers in Deir Mimas, up until the Israeli invasion.

Our village was Christian, and our family was Greek-Orthodox—"Bechara" means "annunciation" in Arabic. At home, Aunt Adlahit took care of our religious education. She was a very pious woman who had thought about taking the holy orders, and although in the end she became a schoolteacher, she was always the nun of the family. I'm not observant, but I still consider her a beautiful picture of religion: open and serene. When Sunday came and it was time for church, Adlahit took us to pray with the Catholics because their parish was closest. But for me, in those days, religion really meant the holy feasts.

Every September 15th we would honor the village patron saint, a hermit named St. Mama. We wouldn't have missed that feast for anything in the world. On that day, all the children who had gone off to study or work in Beirut came home to Deir Mimas. The Becharas, known for our love of a good time, came like the rest. Off in the courtyard of a monastery dedicated to St. Mama, far away, buried deep in the olive groves, we'd eat, dance, and play music the whole night through. It could be quite a time; the men, though not only the men, would usually drink more *arak* than was wise. Finally, at daybreak, we'd get ready for the service and procession. Weddings, too, were times for religion and rejoicing. For seven days and seven nights, nearly the entire village toasted the union of my cousins Michel and Catherine. What an event it was!

They were married in 1976. In our collective memory, it remains the last great village wedding, belonging to that golden age broken by the war, the war which would first divide and then scatter us.

My grandfather Hanna was the living embodiment of this traditional world. His reputation was already well-established in Deir Mimas. He was known as a just man, but severe, often brutally so. One day, without his knowledge, my father's brother, Uncle Nayef, was having some fun—he had perched me, his four-year-old niece, on the kitchen table, and by offering me little sips from a glass of *arak*, was encouraging me to dance. *Arak* was an adult's drink, forbidden to children, but I loved it and loved to dance, so I didn't need much convincing. But the joke was soon over. My grandfather returned unexpectedly, surprising my uncle. After giving me a slap, he chastised my uncle, smashing the glass of liquor to pieces on the ground. I was always afraid of him, and I know I wasn't alone. My grandfather was a man capable of striking any of his children, girl or boy. Even his daughters-in-law were not always safe from his fists. He had been a farmer for most of his life, but in his old age he had found a profession worthy of his character: guarding the vineyards from thieves and gleaners. Hardly anyone dared test his vigilance.

Grandfather Hanna was born at the beginning of the century, and had lived through the French mandate in Lebanon between the wars. Buried at the bottom of his papers was a certificate attesting his loyalty to the occupying power, received during his military service. While my grandmother Salima, obsessed with politics, might fume and rail against some party or other, my grandfather always stayed indifferent, aloof. Yet they shared so many stories, some of which could set them openly against each other. Hanna had always held the south Lebanese landowner Ahmed el-Assaad in high esteem. My grandmother ridiculed the man publicly. She could never forget how, when the villagers of his district had petitioned him for the opening of a school, he had replied haughtily, "My son Kamel attends school, and I consider that quite sufficient." Years later, my grandmother would often act out the scene for us, still as indignant as ever.

My father had left the village at a young age. When my neighbors asked me which of the Becharas was my father, I could see that his name, Fawaz, didn't mean much to them. He rarely visited his parents, unlike my mother, Najat, who had stayed close to her friends and family and took care to see them regularly. Of course, she was able to come to the village much more often than my father. He was forced to stay in Beirut and work when the rest of us—my two older brothers, older sister, and myself—left the city.

Our trips to Deir Mimas were always real expeditions, even in a little country like Lebanon where one seldom travels more than thirty or forty miles.

We didn't, of course, own a car, so we would take our luggage on board one of the collective taxis that traversed the country. Whether for summer vacation or Christmas or Easter holidays, it was always an odyssey. It took nearly three hours for us to rejoin our village, along a road whose twists and turns became more tortuous as we approached the south's rocky escarpments. Our stopping-places were always the same: Saida, to buy pastries, and Nabatiya, for meat. We also brought bread from Beirut, the "modern" bread which I grew up with. I much preferred it to the bread of my grandfather's house, those great flour pancakes cooked under an iron dome, heated by a fire of wood and dried cow-dung.

But things always evened out. We never left Deir Mimas empty-handed, especially not at summer's end. During our holidays, we would plant and pick the fruits and vegetables that grew plentifully and were usually eaten locally. No house lacked its little plot of land, and anything could grow in that generous earth: corn, eggplants, tomatoes, zucchini, onions, thyme. But Deir Mimas' reputation came from the quality of its olives. The olive-harvest kept us busy for long days in October and early November. It was a tradition, an ancestral rite. Our olive oil was some of the best in the country. At home, too, my mother and her sisters-in-law would prepare dried spices and preserves that we would bring back to Beirut, reminding us of our summers in Deir Mimas.

Gathering dead wood from the olive groves was another of our tasks. Everyone worked to feed the kitchen hearth and boil the water for washing, helping my grandparents avoid the cares of winter. The men would regularly prune the olive-trees in order to improve next year's harvest. As a child, I was fascinated by the axe they used to cut the branches and prune the trunks. I would have given anything to use it myself, but it was doubly forbidden, for all children and especially for girls.

And so Deir Mimas was, for a long time, like paradise to me.

While the village was far from Beirut, it was only a short way from the Israeli frontier. A few miles further on the road through town and you reached the first border station. Of course for us, Israel was entirely out of the question. It was impossible to see Israeli land or houses from Deir Mimas; for that, you would have had to scale the ridge that separated us. But above all, I grew up during a very difficult period for the Arab countries, who at that time still hoped to drive the Israelis from all of what had been the British mandate of Palestine. The defeat of 1967, which saw the Israeli Army conquer the West Bank and the Gaza Strip, as well as the Sinai Desert and the Golan Heights, was met with shock and dismay. The Arab armies had already been beaten once in 1948, and had eagerly and actively prepared for revenge. Their disappointment was immense.

And yet, if one chose to follow back the thread of history, it had all started not far from our village. There, the first Jewish colonists supported by Edmund Rothschild had settled on land bought with varying degrees of honesty from the Arabs. In the Israeli village of Metulla, the closest to the border, they keep yellowing old photographs of the people they call "pioneers." I knew nothing of all that. But I heard my grandmother's endless lamentations of the past and her lost land, of the villagers torn from their villages when the state of Israel was created. And over and over again she would describe the atrocities committed by the Israeli troops against Lebanese civilians during the first Arab-Israeli war.

Later, when in 1978 the Israeli Defense Forces (IDF) occupied the south of Lebanon—contravening UN resolutions and in defiance of international law—Israel became a more concrete reality for the people who had remained in Deir Mimas. Many of them tried to find work in Israel, the enemy camp. They could earn much higher wages there than at home. But their lives were hardly easy. Each day they would rise at dawn, enduring meticulous searches and hours of humiliating delays at Israeli border stations, before reaching their workplace, where they would often be forced to labor at a punishing speed. Returning to Lebanon at the end of the day, they would again be forced to wait indefinitely at the border, while the Israeli soldiers, following the mind-numbing rules of security, glared at them suspiciously.

However, in the early 70s, my childhood years, no one in Deir Mimas would have imagined that less than a decade later invasion and then occupation were to be our fate.

It was as if our southern neighbors were hidden from view. Failing to drive them from what had become their land, we had driven them from our minds. In any case, it was no subject for children, and when the grownups discussed serious matters, we were sent to play outside. In that time, the young people went not to the south but to the north to study and find work, to Beirut. With the death of Egyptian President Gamal Abdel Nasser, Beirut had eclipsed Cairo as the most prominent Arab city. Cosmopolitan, intellectual, and rich, it was the beacon of the Middle East. But there were ominous rumblings, and divisions threatened its national unity. The Palestinian cause was the source of much controversy; the PLO had a strong presence in Lebanon after being expelled from Jordan during the Black September crisis of 1970. The divide between the Lebanese right and left grew ever sharper, bringing conflict to the schools, universities and streets. Different organizations were mobilized and the arms trade flourished. The situation was explosive.

Like many others from our village, we lived in a modest place in a southeastern suburb of Beirut called Shiyya. My father and his brothers had moved into a hastily constructed building of five floors. Our apartment was tiny, and the rooms seemed to shrink as the family grew. But on our father's income, we could never imagine moving to a house where we would each have our own room. In any case, we were used to living and sleeping together. When we visited my grandfather in the village, each family shared a single room, and everyone made do. Life was simple like this.

I didn't have much time to get attached to our house in Beirut. When the civil war began in 1975, Shiyya was at the center of the conflict. Rockets and mortars flew above our heads. With its walls riddled with bullets and breached by shells, its rooms looted and empty, our home was branded by the inexorable advance of war. The building was eventually reduced to a state of ruin. We had by this time moved back south, far from Beirut. Life went on in Deir Mimas as if nothing had changed, although my father stayed in the city to work as always, despite the bombs. He described for us the woes of our neighborhood. In our ransacked apartment, he was able to gaze upon the only two books left behind by thieves: the Bible and the Koran. Later on, my uncles tried to move back to their apartments, but to no avail. After a few months, the war again drove them away.

Our building no longer exists. It was torn down along with the surrounding apartments, and I would be hard pressed to point out its exact former location. When I returned to the places of my childhood, I recognized nothing, not the former site of the buildings, nor the open ground where we used to play, broken by a rail line linking Saida in the south with Tripoli to the north.

In the early years of the civil war, the changing times tossed us between Deir Mimas and temporary shelters in Beirut. We were refugees in our own city. Returning to our village once, in 1976, we went straight to a great-aunt's place. Her home, with its lovely garden, seemed so comfortable that I have memories of spending an entire year there, although it was only a few weeks. Before moving into the house in Beirut where my parents still live, we stayed at the home of one of my father's friends who had fled to Syria. There, in the West Beirut neighborhood of Mar Elias, it was calm enough even during the worst times of war. This was simply because no political party had its headquarters nearby, and therefore there were no potential targets.

In September of 1998, when I was freed from Khiam, I returned to that little apartment of two rooms and a terrace. I stay there whenever I come back to Beirut. After the "operation," I was not able to visit Deir Mimas, or any other place in the occupied zone. Nor was any member of my family able to do so, not until the Israeli army retreated from South Lebanon in 2000. It was as if we had been banished.

2 FAMILY

Does one's date of birth have an influence over the events of one's life? Having come into this world on June 15, 1967, I could well ask such a question.

My birthday was a day of defeat for the Arab world. On that day, the armies of Jordan, Egypt, and Syria were put to flight by the IDF. In Cairo, the faltering Gamal Abdel Nasser announced his resignation, leaving his beaten country dumb with shock. I was the youngest child, the baby of the family. My parents had married at the age of twenty in 1958. My brother Adnan was born a year later, followed by my sister Hanan, my brother Omar, and then myself. Perhaps it was as a token of hope that my parents called me Soha, or "star."

Of all the politicians in Lebanon, my favorite was none other than my father. He was a Communist and trade unionist, and had been so probably since his teens. I say "probably" because he didn't drum his beliefs into our ears—quite the contrary. He was a silent man, though always ready to struggle for the cause. Out of respect for his family, he participated in all the religious holidays of the village, and I only discovered his allegiance to the Party much later, when I myself thought of joining its ranks. I never dared ask my father the reasons for his political commitment.

Our village had the reputation of being a stronghold of the left, at least before the Israeli occupation of 1978. It was also a place where children were strongly encouraged to study. School grades were a matter of public knowledge, and they were always higher than in the surrounding villages. My father had been forced to abandon his studies after a dispute with a soldier, but he remained passionately interested in books and learning. He was attracted to the intellectual milieu within the Party, which was particularly prominent towards the end of the 1950s. I would guess that he also supported the Party's doctrine privileging citizenship over religious affiliation.

My father has always worked in printing houses as a compositor or printer. He still goes to work each morning, although he could be enjoying a well-deserved retirement after all those years of war. For him, earning a living remains essential. My childhood memories are of a man totally absorbed by his profession.

I didn't see him much aside from Sundays when we would go out as a family, sometimes to the beach, but more often to visit relatives. Later, the civil war and its accompanying mortar fire made such visits impossible, and my father's political commitment abruptly became wound up with his work. The printing house *Al Hadath*, "The News," had been destroyed at the beginning of the conflict, and my father was hired by *Al Amal*, "Hope," another printer close to the Party. It kept going, through thick and thin, during the whole war, putting out the official Communist paper, *Nidaa* or "The Call." When the fighting chased us away, wrecking our home, we found refuge in an apartment belonging to this printing house.

My mother, blessed with a strong personality, was the head of the household. She was in charge of all decisions regarding the children. When I wanted to go on a hiking trip with some friends from my youth group, she refused permission. I had to wait until she was out of the house before asking my father, who never knew how to say no. Her mood was generally lighthearted, and she was always telling stories and making jokes. She never complained about the hardships of war, neither the cuts in water or electricity that put neighborly relations to the test, nor the bombardments. Unlike my father, she was not interested in politics. I know that in the last elections before the civil war, in 1972, she had voted for the left, but more to make her husband happy than from any deep conviction.

My mother quickly grew to find the Party somewhat invasive.

As a newlywed, she had been forced to pack her bags and follow my father to Syria—he and my uncle had been sent there on a secret mission. A counter-order forced the two militants to return abruptly to Beirut, which meant temporarily abandoning their young brides, each of whom had just had her first child. As the years passed, my mother's resentment against politics, which she wished to keep out of the home, only grew.

Unfortunately for her, our family's reputation was well established. When, in 1982, Bachir Gemayel was elected President of the Republic, his Phalangist supporters in Deir Mimas, where we then lived, came to gloat under our windows. "*Bashar, bashar, bashura, beit Beshara maqura,*" they chanted, "Have you heard the news? The Becharas are getting worried." Indeed, the victory of a right-wing Maronite candidate was a definite setback for the Communists.

From the beginning of the civil war, my parents were aware of the risks of political involvement. Our first taste came in April 1975, when a sniper began to fire from an attic near our first house, near what later became the front lines. He was a Phalangist named Issa. He brought terror to our neighborhood, firing with deadly accuracy. The railroad company suspended train service because of the risk, and to this day it has not resumed. After a month, pro-Syrian militias decided to dislodge the sniper, going through our neighborhood with a fine-toothed comb. My parents realized that we were the only family that didn't own weapons, not even a pistol or a simple hunting rifle. Eventually, Issa was captured. In my imagination, he would be executed in the place where he grew up, hanged as an example in front of all his neighbors. As for us, we had already taken refuge in Deir Mimas.

A short while later, a Phalangist friend of ours came to warn my father that he could be shot in reprisal, a kind of planned, symbolic assassination. My father spent two months barricaded inside the printing house; outside waited the men of Camille Chamoun, leader of another rightist Maronite movement. The printers' owner, Salim el-Laouzi, managed to get my father out in an official car belonging to the presidential palace. My father was lucky. At around the same time, a colleague of his at the printers was gunned down by mistake.

My mother tried to make sure that none of her children were around when my father and his brothers talked politics. She didn't have a chance, at least not so far as my older brother and myself were concerned. Before the civil war began, my brother's school principal, another Phalangist, had struck the fourteen-year-old Adnan for talk judged to be too left-wing. Maybe it ran in the family. My father was not the only one at fault; my uncle Nayef, also a Communist, shared the responsibility. He was younger than my father, and worked with him at the printers.

The atmosphere at my uncle's was completely different than at home. Everyone in his house was involved in politics: himself, of course, but also his wife, Nawal, who was an activist with the Women's Union and a dedicated Party member. I discovered that world in the late seventies. After the Israeli occupation of South Lebanon, I spent nearly all my summer vacations with them. When Uncle Nayef came to pick me up after school, he transported me into another world. It was a hectic life where I could have a hand in everything. My uncle's house was a gathering-place for meetings and discussions. There I would see my uncle Dawud and his wife Jamila, both of them militants. My grandmother would often tell us the story of their legendary wedding: when the family came down to the village to formally ask for Jamila's hand, she was in jail, having been arrested after a demonstration.

In the middle of the chaos of war, Nayef the activist and Nawal the feminist helped me discover political debate, ideals, and the concept of commitment. For this I have always been grateful.

I inherited my father's passion for politics, developing it at his brother's side. I also adopted my father's sense of discretion. A childhood memory has stuck with me. I was watching my brother Omar and a cousin play noisily in our living room. Suddenly, a shoe flew through the air, smashing a window. I ran excitedly to my mother, who was visiting a neighbor. I burst in and breathlessly told the whole story down to the last detail, pointing the finger at the one responsible. Without blinking, my mother asked me to return home and wait for her. I held my tongue, a bit shamefaced. When my mother arrived, she ordered me to go and kneel in the bathroom, giving no reason. Those two hours seemed like an eternity to me. I asked myself what I might have done to deserve such a fate. When my father came home, I burst into tears. He let me get up, and told me to ask my mother the reasons for her punishment. Once again, I swore to her that I was not the guilty party, which only made her even angrier. She finally made it clear to me that one must never tell tales in front of other people—and above all one must never denounce another.

I don't know if it was because of this, but early on I decided never to share my secrets and my deepest feelings, not even with my parents, brothers, and sister, in spite of our closeness and affection.

All of us Bechara children led active lives, but each in his or her own way.

My brother Adnan was a teenager when Lebanon slid into civil war. He knew its difficulties at first hand, living through them all until his departure in 1978. My parents didn't want him close to the conflict, so he left for the security of the Soviet Union, to continue his studies in Kharkov. Because of our modest income, France, or especially America, was out of the question. The USSR was less expensive and more in line with my brother's beliefs. If he studied there, he could get a scholarship from the General Labor Confederation, to which my father belonged. His departure turned out to separate us for good. In Kharkov, he met a young woman, a Greek Cypriot named Tassola, and they were married. After finishing their studies in electrical engineering, they went to live in Cyprus. My brother later returned to Lebanon to look for work. When two of his friends were killed in an explosion, he decided to move permanently to Cyprus, his wife's home.

I learned all this later, after the camp.

My sister Hanan was very different. She was a good student,

and didn't reveal much of herself. Unlike my brother and myself, she was not active in politics. I was her confidante and her alibi when she wanted to go out with her friends and our mother needed convincing. My mother was always reassured if I left with Hanan, or at least if I said that I was going out with her. Whenever I wanted to help my sister, I would say that I was with her. The truth was our secret. Life went on, even during the civil war. My sister was having a serious love affair with our neighbor Pierre. He played the eccentric, which didn't help him much with my parents. But for nights on end, while everyone else slept, from balcony to balcony he would unburden his heart to my sister. After many months, they were finally able to come out in the open and get married.

But I was no longer there. I was in Khiam.

My other brother, Omar, always enjoyed the pleasures of life. He abandoned his studies after high school, preferring to go to work. He too went into printing, becoming a specialist in photo retouching. But his life was also shaken by the war, and it changed course after a bombardment in 1983. On that day, he and my mother took refuge on the second floor of our house. My father, my sister and I were on the third floor—we couldn't make it down in time. The bombs had begun to fall just as Hanan had decided to take a bath. During the bombardment, my mother was seriously injured in the elbow by a mortar blast. She was in the hospital for three months. From that moment on, Omar thought of only one thing: leaving Lebanon. He finally managed it in 1985. Four years later, in exile in West Berlin, he had front-row seats for the fall of the Berlin Wall.

Here again, only the faintest hint of such events reached me in my cell.

In different ways, I took after each of my brothers and my sister. I was the baby of the family, political like Adnan, athletic like Hanan, who was a fitness instructor before studying Arab literature, and I was a lover of life like Omar. I was always interested in sports. I started in track-and-field as a sprinter, and then turned to team sports like basketball and later ping-pong, all while training in gymnastics. Sports gave me a feeling of freedom, which would come in handy in the years to follow.

I also took after my sister in her dedication to her studies. I was a fast learner, and in elementary and high school I was often the first in my class. I was interested in everything, although the natural sciences were my favorite. I focused on my schoolwork, sheltered by my mother from all the tumult that surrounded us. Our apartment was too small for friends to visit, and I didn't go out much, so I was able to spend a lot of time on my homework. My gift for mathematics even helped me early on to become independent from my parents. Starting when I was twelve, I earned pocket money through tutoring. With more students and more income, my success let me be self-sufficient at the age of fourteen. Before that, my brother Omar and my sister had helped me if I needed anything; my brother worked at the printers to make a little money, and my sister was on a scholarship. With my math tutoring, I made something of a name for myself in the neighborhood. My mother was overjoyed. When I was teaching or correcting homework, she thought, at least I wasn't thinking about politics.

At the age of twelve, however, I was elected president by the girls of my class at Fakr al-Din. The school, named after an old prince of Lebanon, was close to the front lines, but still kept up a high academic level. It was one of the best in Beirut, public or private. More than just a school, Fakr al-Din echoed all the political debates that shook the country. Its social life was intense, with non-stop festivals, discussions, and concerts. The school would also show up to every demonstration in Beirut, which was probably why I loved it so much.

Most likely, I was elected class president because I was active in organizing festivals, and because I sometimes represented my year in athletic events. I would often see this law confirmed—responsibility is always given to the most energetic, even if they don't desire it. I never liked to order people around or make decisions for others, but over the years I was increasingly forced to accept this kind of position. This happened to me as an activist in the Union of Democratic Youth, a group tied to the Party which I was involved in around the same time. Practically against my will, I was elected to its National Council a few years later, at a point when I was trying to steer clear of entanglements and keep a low profile.

When I was sixteen, I went for the first time to a scout camp organized by the Union. This meant going against my mother, who was naturally suspicious of this organization because of its connections to the Party. The camp was near the sea, to the south of Beirut. I was in charge of the camping gear, so I came a few days early to make sure everything was ready for our trip. During the final night, the six of us who were there decided to launch a raid against a nearby camp run by another progressive group. I offered to distract the sentry. According to the rules, we were allowed to try and trick the counselors on guard, and capture other scouts or steal equipment. The camp that managed this proved its superiority.

It was midnight. Casually, I strolled over to the sentry, pretending just to have noticed their camp. The guard was a boy. I introduced myself, telling him I was on guard over at the camp run by the Union. I told him he should stretch his legs, and invited him for a tea in our tent. Falling into the trap, he left with me. With him gone and his friends sleeping like logs, my accomplices managed to make off with a tent, three earthenware jars, a chess set, and a hi-fi with speakers.

The next morning, the robbed scouts took some time before noticing that they had been hoodwinked. The alarm was sounded. When the sentry told them what had happened, they sent a party over to our camp. They demanded to see me, but in vain.

Hidden behind a tent, I watched the whole scene. Ali, our leader, generously returned to them the stolen goods, with the exception of the chess set which we kept as a trophy of war. The other camp thought about kidnapping me in revenge, but it was too late. We had already left.

You could call it my first feat of arms.

At the age of six, I discovered war.

I no longer have the child's eyes I saw through then, so my memory is both precise and unreal. I was in Deir Mimas, on vacation.

It was the Saint's day, the festival of Deir Mama, on September 15, 1973. As was our tradition, all my cousins came to stay at my grandparents' house. The songs and laughter of five women and twenty-five children filled the room. Our fathers were working in Beirut. We were supposed to join them the following day, taking our usual roundabout route.

That night was nothing but chaos and noise.

I remember hearing two words: "raids" and "Israelis." The Israeli air force had launched a new offensive against the PLO, who were running guerrilla training camps in the area. The planes came in waves for twelve hours, dropping their bombs not far from the village. We were all much too agitated to sleep. My mother and her sisters decided to distract us by baking bread. The supplies were meant for our trip to Beirut, but they fell prey to our restlessness—we ate them all up during that sleepless night.

When we climbed aboard the car the next day, we learned that the main road was blocked only a few minutes drive from the village. The Israeli bombs had targeted the Khardali Bridge, which spanned the Litani river, linking the South to the rest of the country. It was an unusual wooden bridge, and the sound of vehicles crossing it would cast a unique echo. I can still hear its "voice" ringing in my ears. It was one of the many little landmarks that dotted our voyage. Without the bridge, we had to cross the Bekaa Plain to the east before reaching Beirut, adding two hours to our trip.

The Khardali Bridge was never rebuilt. We found other routes to Deir Mimas, but that particular gap was never filled.

The war caught up with me again two years later, in the city of my birth. Clashes between Israelis and Palestinians had become frequent, but now there was fighting between Lebanese factions. We were caught at home during the first night of gunfire. It was most likely April 13, 1975, the date usu-

3 WAR

ally marked as the beginning of the civil war. We were living in our first apartment, in the neighborhood near Shiyya called Gallery Semaan. We took shelter from the bombing with a neighbor. Rocket fire lit up the sky. Although it was forbidden, I stuck my head out the window to see the flares and the cones of flame rising from the presidential palace not far from our house. It seemed like a marvelous show. We slept huddled together in a crowded room, and this unexpected and unusual situation delighted me. But the adults were in a daze, their eyes filled with fear. They kept telling us not to be afraid, while they were the ones who seemed worried. To keep up their courage, they told each other it would be better tomorrow, all this would soon end and things would go back to normal.

They could not have known that this night would last nearly fifteen years.

The weeks passed, bringing new flare-ups of violence. I learned first-hand the relentless uncertainty of bombs over a city—always blind to civilians.

One of my early memories is from June that same year, at the end of the school term. We had just been given our report cards when the fratricidal war broke out again, ending the graduation ceremony in disarray. We ran from the school towards our house. A rumbling split the sky. Airplanes. My friends pointed at them; they could be seen quite clearly. They were releasing odd-shaped objects over the city. Suddenly I remembered my mother warning me never to touch toys found in the streets or open fields. A radio report had told us the Israelis had been setting booby-traps in the south. I ran, yelling back to my cousin not to touch anything and to hurry home. Behind us, I saw a body puffed out by an explosion, wounded or dead I couldn't tell.

Today I can't even be sure if I really witnessed this scene, or if, after seeing it on television, it became intertwined with the most vivid images of my childhood.

From that year on, school followed the irregular rhythm of war. The first few times that classes were interrupted by fighting, no one understood what was happening. Why did the teachers break off a lesson all of a sudden? Why were our parents here at school in the middle of the morning? Why were they taking us away? These questions had no logical answers. It was a time when we would stop work without knowing when we'd start again. We would never walk home alone, and often we'd wait for our parents to come to the school and pick us up. Every day I had the same fear: that no one would come and get me, that I would be left alone in the middle of the bombs. All the children felt the same way, even though they would laugh about it just seconds after finally seeing their mother or father. For a long time, the school year never ended when it was supposed to. We never knew each morning if the day would pass without incident. Sometimes, report cards would abruptly be handed out. A term would end early, cut short by yet another battle between allied factions turned mortal enemies.

The year was 1977. We had moved into a new apartment. For convenience's sake, I was still going to the school where I had enrolled in September, Mar Mikhael, close to the front lines. Because it was a bit far from our new home, my mother thought it simpler for me to take a hired car to school. It was a large gray Mercedes, driven by a taciturn man in his forties. After school he would pick me up and then drop me in front of our building.

We were driving home one afternoon, the usual five passengers in the car. Halfway there, we were caught in an exchange of artillery fire at the edge of the Palestinian refugee camp of Sabra, near where the driver was supposed to drop off two students. Dust and uproar filled the streets. Around us was panic. A bomb exploded just behind us, another in front. Everyone in the car was screaming. The ground shook. There were wounded, maybe dead. People ran shouting in all directions, drivers honked in panic and accelerated, trying to clear a path though the fray. Our car skid between shell holes and fallen obstacles. That day was one of the most dangerous I lived through in Beirut. We were lucky—the driver was able to get us home in one piece.

My parents knew nothing of this. I was never talkative when it came to my own life, and kept silent about that terrifying ride home.

When the war began, it quickly imposed its laws, and for every law we had a ritual. First of all, we had to protect ourselves as well as possible. In any room, we were soon able to pick out the best spot to take shelter from the bombs—a place with at least two walls to block rocket fire. Our first apartment lacked even this poor protection; on the contrary, it was particularly exposed to the bombs. We were often forced to stay at our neighbor's on the same floor, an improvised arrangement that could drag on for several nights. But routine soon won out over safety, and we no longer worried about finding shelter. We quickly became experts in stocking food and supplies. Eventually we learned about weapons, the different types, calibers, and origins of each. We could recognize the sound of a rocket or an automatic weapon.

War also brought its side effects. There was the crackle of special radio bulletins when hate and violence drove the fighting to a peak. Each faction had its own radio station, and it was easy to decode the broadcasts when you knew what they were talking about. Cuts to water and electricity also became the rule. We learned to manage, which really meant to do without. We perfected our techniques as the war settled in. For lighting, over the years we switched from candles to kerosene to gas, following the "trends" forced on us by speculators. Finding drinking water was a serious problem, too. The pressure was too low for water to reach the upper floors. The humming of pumps became a constant sound. They drew from tanks—bigger and bigger as the war progressed—on the ground floor, feeding the pipes and then replenishing the reserves when the cuts lasted several days. As sure as war brings death, I learned that it also brings inequality. With their powerful generators and pumps, the rich wanted for nothing. The poor, on the other hand, had to steal electricity from lines still in service. The illicit splicing of electrical wires spread like a giant spider web over the streets of Beirut.

The fighting also had its own vocabulary. After a few weeks we learned about "snipers," "displaced persons," and "refugees"—people like us who had lost their homes to the bombs. Later, when South Lebanon was marked off by Israel and then occupied by its army to protect its northern frontier, the number of refugees shot into the tens of thousands. There was a tradeoff between those who fled the fighting in Beirut, abandoning their homes, and those from the South who came to live in them, penniless and without hope. The refugees discovered city life, with its hitherto unimagined apartment buildings and elevators. We were thrown into the same state when we lost our house, but my father always resisted the temptation to move into an abandoned apartment, even for a few days.

The hosts of cars that fled the war zones, bristling with packages, were refugees too. When we left our first apartment, we brought along our refrigerator and washing machine as well as several pieces of furniture, including two beds and a few chairs. The poor things landed in Deir Mimas, where they were put aside awaiting our return. They ended up following us everywhere in our exile, worn-out strays just like their owners. They were displaced objects, incongruous refugees tied to a car roof or locked in a trunk. They, too, suffered real losses and "deaths" by bombs or by fire.

We took refuge in Deir Mimas during the first few months of civil war. Many had the same reflex, and the village swelled with the return of her children. Each managed to find a home with his or her respective family, some more easily than others. I went to a little school in Deir Mimas, while my brothers and sister went to one a few miles away in Marjayoun. Far from the fray, we spent a wonderful year in our village, the last for quite some time.

I was, however, deeply altered by one event during our stay: the murder of our neighbor Laure by her son Semaan. It was in no way political. Laure was very beautiful, and her free manner was the subject of much gossip. Semaan took a rifle and shot her, trying to avenge the supposedly tainted honor of his family. At that very moment I was looking after her younger son Ibrahim, who was mentally disabled. I was the first to see Laure's body. It was all covered in blood. She was the first dead person I had ever seen up close.

Even apart from this drama, war did not spare our peaceful haven. In 1978, two years after our return to Beirut, Israel decided to invade South Lebanon to push back the PLO. Helicopters dropped leaflets on Deir Mimas calling on its inhabitants to leave. There was an ultimatum announcing that the bombing would start at four the next morning. Most of the villagers fled to safety in the mountains, the Christians easily finding shelter with their Muslim compatriots. Only a few villagers, at most twenty, clung to their homes. A good many of the refugees returned some time later.

But from that point on, Deir Mimas was a village occupied by the Israeli army.

Back in Beirut in the fall of 1976, we again grew used to the conflict. The fragile ceasefires were our only respite—the daily reality was war. War smoothed over and clouded the passing years; I have trouble telling them apart. It turned that time into a jumble of shouts and roars. Often, it brought moments of absurd surprise. One beautiful afternoon I was sitting with my sister on our balcony, mechanically looking out at an artillery battery set up a few hundred yards from our house. The cannon's black mouth seemed to swing in our direction. A bit nervous, I pointed it out to my sister, who annoyedly told me I was seeing things. But the gun was indeed being aimed, and I realized that our little cluster of houses was the target. I barely had time to cry a warning to my sister when an explosion ripped through the air. A shell smashed into a fortunately empty house nearby—a simple error in targeting.

I experienced the fighting differently as I grew older. Through the Union of Democratic Youth, I became an extra in the war's interminable tragedy. The Red Cross and Red Crescent had organized relief squads to help the wounded or those who had nothing and slept in the streets. With the Union, I went further, often helping out in clinics set up in Party-controlled areas, doing the laundry or treating the lightly wounded. Although young people such as myself couldn't really be called Communists, we were considered by the fighters to be militants like them.

You didn't look for action in the civil war, but it caught up with you.

In 1984 I would go regularly to an outpost set up in a former "Young Pioneers" club called Nadi al-Rouad. The bombs were flying between East and West Beirut, and my journey was not without danger. Two snipers had dug in on either side of a necessary crossing point. In order to pass, we somehow had to make an appointment with a "runner," a friend who at a designated moment would wave a piece of clothing to distract the gunmen. During this brief second, the ambulance had to clear the danger zone. We made sure to duck our heads as we clung to its side.

Having reached Nadi al-Rouad, the Pioneers Club, I would do my usual cleaning and chores. A militiaman told me one day how they used the radio to communicate between different posts. Everything was in numbered code—speaking normally was out of the question. Just at that moment, a bomb went off close to the club. A militia fighter for the Socialist Party had been killed. In the blink of an eye the outpost was emptied. The special telephone rang. Mechanically, I answered. The director in charge of the general area was doing a routine check on positions held by the Party. Forgetting security protocol, I eagerly gave all the details of what had just taken place. This impudence made the voice on the other line choke with fury and exasperation. My supervisor came into the room and interrupted the disaster; he was later penalized for such lack of discipline.

A new dispute between Lebanese factions drove me, once again, into that inglorious battle. This time the Party was fighting Amal, the Shiite Muslim movement. I was in charge of staffing a first-aid post. As the fighting reached its peak, many young members of the Union came to work shifts at the post, relieving each other. My two friends and I were the only ones to stay through the whole crisis, treating minor wounds there on the premises. We had no rest for three days and three nights. There were fifteen combatants in our care, since the Amal militia would regularly search the larger clinics looking for their enemies. When they found one, his fate was sealed—they would shoot him on the spot.

In the first-aid post I was in charge of medication, making sure that it was administered according to prescription. With my friends, I also took care of the cooking and cleaning. Tension kept us awake. After seventy-two hours, the situation turned against the Party, and the order was given to evacuate. We erased all traces of activity inside the post, and returned home. For once, my mother was understanding and didn't complain about this strain on my normal life.

She had no idea of the dangers I met, the risks I ran.

While I served with the Union, I was more or less requisitioned to accompany a seriously wounded Socialist Party leader to the American Hospital. He was first treated in a nearby clinic called al-Turk, but his condition called for a transfer to a better-equipped station. The area was riddled with snipers and the Socialists needed a guide—they didn't know how to reach the American Hospital without trouble. We took the Union's ambulance, followed by cars piled with the leader's bodyguards. Obeying what had become a necessary rule when transporting an important personage, our siren's wail was joined by the firing of the bodyguards' kalashnikovs and the blaring of their car horns.

In a whirlwind we passed unharmed through the danger points. There were three of us in the ambulance: the driver, the nurse, and myself. I held the wounded man on his stretcher while we drove at breakneck speed. The driver knew the landmarks by heart, but tension clouded his judgment. We were supposed to do a short stretch on a street which opened onto a checkpoint held by Amal, turning quickly to the right before they had time to react. When the driver reached the crossroads, instead of swinging to the side, he went straight ahead. In front of us, the militiamen, on the alert, moved into a firing position. As one of them aimed a B7 bazooka, we screamed at the driver to turn. Our tires screeched as we swerved into an alleyway, and luckily the shot exploded down an empty street.

But what use is luck when war descends into madness?

In 1981, an assassination near the Arab University of Beirut killed my cousin Marwan. Of all the car bombings to bloody the hate-divided capital, it was one of the deadliest.

Marwan, the son of my Uncle Dawud, was only visiting Lebanon; he was studying in the Soviet Union. But it was his birthday, and he had planned to meet some friends and relatives in a restaurant to celebrate. He had just arrived when the bomb exploded, leveling everything around it. My cousin was not close to the car but was caught in the powerful blast. He fell, his head blown off.

Soon enough, the newsflashes tore through the city. I still remember hearing the bulletin, and I remember my family's anxiety. Everyone in Beirut, after every explosion, wondered frantically about their loved ones, where they were, if they had been on or near the blood-spattered street. If they had, a desperate search for news began, looking through the morgues, hoping not to see the face or body of a loved one. As the assassinations spiraled out of control and became ever deadlier, the morbid task of identification became more difficult. Bodies were often blown to bits, pulverized by the brute force of the bombs. Parents and friends had to be satisfied with miserable tokens, a shred of cloth or paper, to help them come to grips with the unimaginable.

For our family, hope fled that day. The shattering news of Marwan's death lowered onto us a heavy cloak of grief.

4 POLITICS

War is madness.

In Lebanon, like anywhere else, it had its own skewed and perverted logic. I gradually discovered the names it bore: Israelis, Palestinians, Lebanese Right and Left. Abstract names that would progressively become flesh and blood, massacred human beings. The machine-gunned bus at Ain Rummane, the victims mostly Palestinian. The slaughter at Safra Marina, a seaside resort turned into the headquarters of Camille Chamoun's party. The cleansing of the Tal Zaatar refugee camp, emptied of its Palestinian, Shiite, and Leftist Christian inhabitants. Also the deadly assassination of the family of the President of the Republic, Suleiman Franjieh. On top of this: the kidnappings on all sides, the checkpoints springing up everywhere, the city split in two as we looked on, stupefied.

Beirut no longer existed. The name was heard, on the radio and in our conversation, only when qualified by the word East or West.

For more than thirty years, history had weighed on us. Now it began to crush us.

Some background: the Israel-Lebanon border had been relatively quiet between 1949 and 1967, but after that date things began to change. The PLO, using Lebanon as a base, started to increase its operations on Israeli soil. Lebanon suffered brutal reprisals, endless raids and bombardments—later, as a little girl in Deir Mimas, I would learn about this first-hand. The new turn of events caused relations between the PLO and the Lebanese government to deteriorate. The two parties signed an accord in Cairo in 1969, reducing the PLO's room to maneuver but reaffirming their right to resistance, even when acting from Lebanese territory. The accord did nothing to help reduce hostilities along the border, and it became extremely tense and remained so for a long time. Added to this was a similar crisis—Black September—between the PLO and Jordan that degenerated into all-out war, causing the whole Palestinian military apparatus to be evacuated to Lebanon.

So the Palestinians were quite present in Lebanon, whether as a military force or as refugees from the wars of 1948 and 1967. Many Palestinian refugee camps were set up near Beirut, and the Lebanese authorities watched them closely.

The Israelis quickly moved into my imagination after all my grandmother's stories and the bombings of 1973. But the Palestinians stayed on the outskirts. For a long time I had no Palestinian friends. I knew that they had been driven from their land and hoped one day to return, but apart from that, my image of them was blurred and confused. I didn't know about the refugee camps, and I was not particularly moved by the Palestinian cause. Actually, I thought of them like any other Lebanese, and the name Yasser Arafat was not especially familiar to me.

In 1976, at the beginning of the civil war, a murky event cast a pall for quite some time on my vision of this group: the murder of a cousin of mine, apparently killed by Palestinians. One of my father's relatives was driving south from West Beirut with his young son, Afif. They were stopped at a checkpoint at Kfar Tibnit, near Nabatiya. Their papers were requested. The religion marked on their identity cards attracted notice: Greek Orthodox, in other words "Christian. " It had been some time since the PLO and the Christian militias had spoken other than through the exchange of fire—the dirty war was in full swing. Afif was a soldier in the Lebanese Army and did not in the least look like a Phalangist. He thought of himself as on the left, and therefore pro-Palestinian. The militiamen were not interested in such fine distinctions—a Christian could only be an enemy. They brutally dragged my cousin from the car. His mother, understanding what was happening, threw herself at the feet of the men and begged their mercy—but in vain. Afif was coldly executed, a sacrificial victim in a conflict which was not his.

Later, much later, I learned the truth. Afif was killed not by Palestinians, but by a Lebanese Shiite Muslim looking to avenge his brother, who had supposedly been murdered by Phalangists. The man believed his brother had been assassinated, and the people of his village, falling prey to rumors, thought the killing had been done by "foreigners." In fact, the story has an appalling epilogue. The missing brother had himself joined the Phalangist camp and was doing dirty work on their behalf.

I truly encountered the Palestinians a year later, in very different circumstances. Once again, they surrounded the remains of a member of my family: Khalid, the son of one of my father's cousins. But this time, they formed a guard of honor around a martyr's coffin. After the Israeli military intervention in the south, young Lebanese men began to join the *fedayin* to fight the invaders. My cousin was one of them; he had signed up for a Palestinian unit. During an arms transport operation, Khalid stepped on a mine. One of his legs was torn off by the blast. He was evacuated by his companions, but the wounds proved fatal. The PLO decided to pay homage to him with a special funeral. They organized a huge demonstration in West Beirut not far from our house. I watched the ceremony from afar, an observer. I was transfixed by the spectacle in front of me—the young Palestinians marching in rhythm bearing the photos of their martyrs, throwing flowers across streets bedecked with the four colors of Palestine: black, white, red and green.

I discovered a flag, a cause, a people.

During the same period, Israel was setting up its own militia, a proxy army which would later become the South Lebanon Army (SLA). In fact, the Lebanese Christian military men were given direct aid. An officer named Saad Haddad united them all under his command, and with Israel's protection he tried to take control of the border enclaves. They used all kinds of tricks to win the populace to their cause. I remember the murder of a country doctor and his driver, which was presented by the future "collaborators" as an anti-Christian act fomented by Muslims. Actually, it was the result of an argument over money between the driver and a Shiite Muslim. The doctor was murdered because he had witnessed the grim settling of scores between the two men.

Tensions were rising in the village. It was finally incorporated into the "security zone" marked out by the IDF on our land. The new border was not airtight—my mother continued to make regular trips to the village as she had always done. But she was one of the few members of the family able to keep up this tenuous link with our relatives, who now lived under an occupying power.

After the spring of 1975, the fighting between Israel and the PLO became intertwined with the Lebanese civil war. The civil war came after a long period of intermittent conflict, which had progressively chipped away at the country's political structure and institutions. In the West, the war was often presented as a contest between Christians and Muslims, but my family, along with many others, did not experience it this way. In my case, I understood it by using another duality: the right against the left. On the right were of course those parties described as Christian, Pierre Gemayel's Phalange and Camille Chamoun's National Liberal Party, primarily supported by the Maronite community. But we Greek Orthodox were no less Christian, and we were generally allied with the opposing camp.

The left, as the adults at home said, consisted of the Communist and Socialist parties, allied with the PLO, and finally a few Lebanese Muslim organizations—at least this was true at the beginning of the conflict. The two sides were joined by Syria, whose support fluctuated between them. Damascus played the two camps against each other, ensuring an "equilibrium" for its own gain. New parties also came out of the civil war. They were mostly Shiite Muslim, reflecting the increasing demographic weight of this section of Lebanese society: Musa Sadr's Movement of the Disinherited, Amal, and much later,

Hezbollah.

Our daily life was marked by unnatural alliances, internal divisions, and shifting fronts.

After a few years, partially because of the immense advantage it brought to a few profiteers and traffickers, the war began to fuel itself, losing sight of the political disputes that had provided the original spark. This was particularly true after the exit of the Palestinian forces, who were driven from Beirut by the Israeli Army during Operation "Peace in Galilee."

To our misfortune, the madness of war immediately swept up our own army, which supposedly existed to defend and protect us from foreign attacks. The army, unable to stay above polemics and political and military disputes, stubbornly reflected the most suicidal qualities of Lebanese society. Military men took sides, forgetting their duty as protectors of the country as a whole. They plunged into war, choosing one camp or another. This quickly splintered them into small bands in the service of the warlords who would reign over the wreckage of Beirut.

Early on, I realized that the fratricidal conflict was just a tremendous mess, the whole civil war nothing but an enormous fraud. This feeling became concrete when I worked for the civil defense, or the Lebanese Red Cross or Red Crescent. When we treated the wounded and took them to the hospital, we never checked their papers or their religious affiliation. As parties in the civil war, members of all sides were unimpressive. They cared only for details and nursed an incredible energy for trifles while missing the main point.

At the Union of Democratic Youth, our incomprehension led us into discussions that would go on for days. I loved the atmosphere there, although my mother looked unkindly on my going. She had long since lost any illusions about the political commitment of her Communist husband. She was firmly convinced that the Union was nothing but a brainwashing machine, a propaganda tool for an organization that drove her mad. She also thought the Scout Camps were just a cover, a place to indoctrinate young and docile Lebanese and train them in the use of weapons. She would thunder at my father:

"What good does it do, the Party? Nothing! Always the same old stories!" She never waited for a response—as always, he stayed silent.

No one would dream of denying that the Union was quite close to the Party. But in contrast to my mother's fears, the Union was above all a source of energy and questions, of doubt and spirit. In any case, I was not a card-carrying Communist. I lent a hand now and then in the shelters they ran, but I still hung on to my own opinions and freedom of action. I was not a militant, just attached to an organization to which my whole little world—my father and uncles—belonged. Because of this, I had an ambiguous relationship to the Lebanese Communist Party. I was something of a "fellow traveler," though at the time I didn't know this expression nor what it implied. I was an observer, hesitating to get involved. But I recognized myself in those ideals. They had been ground under the wheels of war, but my father embodied them daily by my side. Of course, I knew the Communists made mistakes in the heat of battle, but this did nothing to dim the light of conviction that shone for me in my father's eyes.

What exactly was the ideal that attracted me to such an organization? Not the class struggle, although this was one reason for the Party's involvement in the war. Paradoxically, it was the idea of nationhood. The Party had never sought to slice Lebanese society up by religion. It had always spoken and continued to speak of a country for all, with each citizen having equal rights and duties. It was a national, even republican perspective, and it touched me deeply, waking parts of me long numbed by fratricidal slogans and rallying cries. I accepted it instinctively with all my being. I was not a Lebanese Christian— I was first of all Lebanese, and then from a Greek Orthodox family.

As the 1980s began, after five years of fighting, something had become clear to me. Lebanon had only one real enemy, one occupying power: the state of Israel. To my mind, the civil war was just a consequence of this situation. As I saw it, the Israeli authorities had kept up the same strategy for decades, and their decision to occupy the south of Lebanon grew naturally from it. This was to continue expanding Israel's borders. I thought their aim was clear: to cause Lebanon to disintegrate, then to seize additional land, strengthening Israel's core by enlarging its reach.

This threat stirred up many a teenage discussion, at least when we weren't just coping with the effects of the war's confused rhythm on our studies and hopes for the future. Ever since childhood, we had been nursed on Marcel Khalifé's patriotic songs, which my brothers sang tirelessly. They were just as strong for me as the plays of Ziad el-Rahbani, that unsparing seeker of democracy. His satirical writings were famous for skewering the fanaticism of some of his fellow citizens. His most cutting tirades were often quoted on the radio or at school, denouncing the shifting games and string-pulling that led Lebanon from one abyss to another.

In 1980, at the age of thirteen, I went for the first time to a festival of political songs at the UNESCO headquarters in Beirut. The night of Marcel Khalifé's concert, the hall was full to bursting. My cousins had convinced my brother Omar, my sister, and me to come with them. We arrived an hour before the show, but already there were hardly any seats left. The singer had barely stepped on stage when the crowd started to wave red flags, handkerchiefs, and pieces of clothing. Swept away by the moment, I took off my jacket—it was red—and held it in the air. After this moment of euphoria had passed, I started listening to the words. They were stronger than any political speech. Without making distinctions between Lebanese and Palestinians, Marcel Khalifé sang the pain of one who had lost his land and home, and who drowned himself in despair. He sang nostalgically of the tobacco fields of South Lebanon, abandoned during the war. He sang the story of Khiam, bombed in 1978 by the Israeli Air Force and then looted by militias. I don't remember hearing any hymns in praise of any particular community. I remember only poems sung for Lebanon, our land, our home.

Yet at the university a few years later, I was able to see just how deeply the divisions in our country ran. With the Iranian revolution of 1979, the new Islamist movement was in full swing in the Middle East—Beirut included. There was even a muted rivalry between Hezbollah, which was backed by Iran, and Amal, supported by Syria. Hezbollah's militants set themselves to postering verses in Persian from the Koran, while Amal held that the Holy Book had been written once and for all in Arabic. Strict codes of dress began to crop up. The Islamist movement brought with it unbearable excesses: intellectuals were assassinated or kidnapped, women at the beach thought to be indecently dressed were showered with abuse. Since I was close to the Communists, I was a target. I embodied a sociability they would have liked to forbid, with all my athletic activity. I was also mad about chess, and loved to play with friends from high school and university. Because of all this, I received death threats from some young members of Amal.

The situation was absurd. At that time, I did not even rule out the possibility of joining their ranks, in order to better struggle for the cause of resistance.

5 THE INVASION

I have never celebrated my birthday.

Especially not on June 15, 1982, when I turned fifteen. Celebrating anything was out of the question. We were getting ready to leave our house for another exile in the South. Our enemies had arrived—the Israelis had made their camp, triumphant, at the gates of my city.

It had all started a few days earlier, in London. During the night of June 3, the Israeli ambassador to England, Shlomo Argov, was seriously wounded in an assassination attempt. The Israelis immediately blamed the PLO, despite the latter's disavowal and condemnation of the perpetrators. As usual, there were massive reprisals in South Lebanon, and in response the PLO bombed the Upper Galilee. At the urging of Lebanon, the Security Council tried to get the two parties to accept a ceasefire, but in vain. On June 5, General Ariel Sharon ordered his armored divisions into my country.

Operation "Peace in Galilee" had begun.

In Beirut, the early signs of the invasion were no cause for panic. It wasn't the first time that Israel had made incursions into Lebanese territory. We didn't realize the danger, in spite of the unusual methods employed by the invaders. Most Lebanese politicians were sure that the Israelis would move into the South to "clean out" pockets of likely Palestinian resistance, but then promptly fall back to their lines of defense, leaving the local militias they supported to act as a buffer.

Yet for over a year, pessimists like the Communist Party had warned of a massive invasion designed to settle the score with the Palestinians for good. The evidence soon proved them

right. As the hours passed, we became witness to the unthinkable. The IDF would take up a position, and then move further.
Advance forces brought by sea moved to cut off the *fedayin* and
their allies, closing in on them from two sides. The Beaufort
Castle, near Deir Mimas, fell into their hands. Ignoring a few
pockets of resistance, the armored columns climbed north,
unstoppable, toward Beirut.

In the west half of the city, we Lebanese began to pull ourselves together and prepare, without fully believing it possible,
for a potential siege. For months the shelling between East and
West had shaped our lives, but the advance of the Israelis made
our situation for the first time unbearable. There was often no
bread to be had, and the hospitals were filled to overflowing.
There were shortages of nurses and beds. At the urging of the
Red Cross, my friends from the Union and I found ourselves
working in a school requisitioned to serve as a hospital. The
tension grew as the Israeli tanks closed in.

For the first time, I was face to face with my enemy.

It was a staggering idea, and it left me torn between fear and
defiance. Everyone had dug themselves into shelters. As the
bombs fell, I played basketball with my friends, and when the
alert sounded and the streets emptied suddenly, I would continue slowly and deliberately on my way.

The fight did not turn out to be an equal one. The con-
frontations were brief between the Israeli troops and the
Palestinian and allied Lebanese forces. The IDF advanced
inexorably, a steamroller. As they came under Syrian fire, they
revealed their strength. Skirmishes increased daily, and Israel
always had the upper hand. Damascus' air force suffered heavy
losses and practically abandoned Lebanese airspace. On the
ground, the hopeless Syrian divisions were entirely routed.
Israeli forces attacked Khalde—the key to Beirut—in the west,
but without success. The pressure rose. Eventually, the Israeli
troops skirted the city to the east and entered almost without a
fight through the Phalangist-controlled sector. West Beirut was
caught in a vice, enduring heavy bombardments from the
Israeli naval and air forces. In our neighborhood, the ground

shook with every impact.

On June 14, the night before my birthday, we were in effect surrounded.

My uncle took charge of getting us away from the fighting. My father felt unable to leave Beirut, but he was equally unwilling to leave his family in such danger. My mother, too, felt it was impossible to stay. On June 27 and 28, leaflets were dropped on West Beirut. Like the ones in Deir Mimas a few years earlier, they advised all civilians who wished to survive to leave immediately. A huge exodus swept West Beirut, and against my will I was dragged along with it. Of course, not everyone was in the same boat—some had been rich enough to have already left the city, by plane or in their personal cars. The Palestinians were naturally left behind, but also the poorest Lebanese, and those who had no other refuge elsewhere in the country.

Our departure rent me in two. We had fled, surrendered, accepted defeat. I protested with all my strength. I wanted to stay—to stay right up until the end. I wanted to stay in my home.

My mother, who was getting ready to leave our house, would have nothing to do with my teenage stubbornness. She bluntly ordered me to follow her, along with my sister, my brother, and my Uncle Subhi. We had to leave. I managed to gain one paltry concession: we would not sleep in East Beirut, although we would have to drive through it. It was where our Israeli enemies had passed, and its inhabitants had allowed them to take the city.

I had not set foot in East Beirut for a long time. We crossed the demarcation line, which had been opened toward the West to cement the invasion. I watched from the back seat as we made it through the terrible Museum Crossing, near the French Embassy, which was still off-limits to Palestinians. On the other side lay a different world. While West Beirut had been destroyed by bombs, the part controlled by the Phalangists seemed almost untouched. I had just left a city ravaged by war, but a few hundred yards away was this staggeringly banal universe—a normal city of shops, pedestrians, and crowded cafés.

We had left in a state of disarray after days of bombardments, so to take our minds off things my mother offered to take us shopping for new clothes. Trapped inside my rage, I was not at all tempted.

The evacuation was delayed. We were forced to sleep in that zone of disgrace, a relative's place. I chewed over my anger late into the night. I was furious at the whole world, furious at the Lebanese who had let the Israelis into my city and who were no longer real Lebanese to me. But I was also angry at my family; they had chosen to flee, perhaps for a long time.

This time, I was afraid we had left for good.

The next day we piled into a white Peugeot—ten of us in a car meant for five—and left. We knew that the way would be blocked by Israeli checkpoints. As soon as the first one came in sight, my uncle made us tear up our papers. He even made me destroy my Lebanese Red Cross card. My protests were in vain—he was unyielding. Each checkpoint was another test, its own particular humiliation. They spoke to us in Arabic, examining us again and again. We waited under the hot sun, often for hours, without anything to drink. At one place, a baby was crying. He was thirsty. His parents pleaded with a soldier for a glass of water, but the soldier refused.

Moving slowly, our car circled the city to the south. We passed by a beach where Israeli soldiers sunbathed in swimsuits. They seemed quite at home.

After an eight-hour drive we arrived in Deir Mimas. It was the first time in nearly five years that I had returned. Seeing my family—my aunt and my grandparents—filled me with emotion. I also saw before me an army that seemed to be Lebanese. There was not a shadow of an Israeli soldier. But these men who carried guns and wore the national uniform were, I would later learn, in the employ of the Jewish State. I was struck by the rampant colonization of the village by Israeli products. Everyone wore the military fatigues made by our enemies and given away for free. Their soft drinks and food products were everywhere.

I spontaneously decided to boycott everything that came

from there.

The atmosphere in the village was heavy. It was split in two: those for and those against, the allies and the enemies of Israel. The exodus from the capital had brought back some left-wing families, like ours, who had been gone since 1978. But it also brought other young people, from East Beirut, who were sympathetic to the Phalangist movement.

After a few days, the Phalangists of the village, thinking the tide was with them, tried to open a headquarters. Their efforts were soon cut short—the Israelis would tolerate no political force other than their ally, Saad Haddad. Soon any propaganda that might increase tensions was forbidden. Somehow or other, two Lebanons lived side by side in Deir Mimas. Each one forced itself to avoid controversial subjects, and people had to be satisfied with talking about insignificant things. Phalangists and Communists even went to the same athletic club, created for that purpose.

We stayed in the village until the end of November. I tried to use my stored-up anger in my studies, but I could not stop thinking about Israel and my duty as a Lebanese. I was overwhelmed with joy by the creation, on September 16, of a united Resistance Front. Finally, a glimmer of hope. It sprang up just after the assassination of Israeli ally Bashir Gemayel, who had opened the gates of Lebanon to the IDF, putting civilians in danger. He was killed by a bomb just after being designated President of the Republic. I lamented the manner in which he was killed, but the news of his death consoled me.

Bashir Gemayel's rise to power had electrified the Phalangists. They were the ones who had shouted their joy under our windows. His death was met by mourning and distress by part of Deir Mimas—but by one part only.

After a few weeks, my father joined us in the village. He had been sorely tested by the siege of Beirut. He and two of his friends were the only ones who had remained in our neighborhood. Together they had lived through Black Sunday—the 24-hour nonstop bombardment of West Beirut. Despite the fire pouring from the sky, my father was caught up in his work. For a while he had nothing to eat or drink. Sick and exhausted, he was finally rescued by my uncle. My father spoke in his own particular style—words almost had to be dragged from his mouth. Little by little, he described to us the worst times of the siege. He told us how he and his friends had managed to meet the challenge of publishing the paper each day. He also told us about the departure of the Palestinian soldiers on August 30. They were escorted by the blue-helmeted UN peacekeepers; an internationally-organized agreement between the Israelis and Yasser Arafat had brought them in.

My father described how tears, dejection, and stifling silence fell on Beirut. The Palestinians, our brothers, hated by part of the population, had been defeated. They were to leave their temporary refuge and set off once more for the unknown. For once, according to my parents, the country was of one mind. At that moment my mother was with my father in Beirut, and I knew how suspicious she was of Yasser Arafat. But this time I heard her express an unusual compassion towards the Palestinian leader and his people. For many, a page had turned. But as for myself, I knew in my heart of hearts that the Palestinians' departure had solved nothing. It was clear to me that the Israelis had used them as a pretext, exploiting our divisions to move even more securely into Lebanon.

My father saved his strongest words to describe Sabra and Shatila, the refugee camps south of the city where Palestinians had been massacred. The victims of this slaughter numbered in the thousands, while the Israelis, who controlled access to the camps, had stood by and watched. All the Lebanese parties as well as Arafat put the blame on Israel and its allies: the militias of Saad Haddad, the Lebanese Forces, and the Phalangists.

For a few weeks, my father stayed with us and gathered his strength. He took advantage of a rare opportunity: the opening of the Israeli border. He and my mother were for the first time permitted to cross into enemy territory, officially to visit a relative in East Jerusalem. It was obviously a public relations exercise on the part of Israel, an attempt to drive a wedge between Lebanese living in the South and those in Beirut. In East

Jerusalem, my father labored to convince the Palestinians that he shared their ideas and that not all Lebanese had been sold to the Israelis. It took me a while to understand how he had long been tempted, as a committed Communist, by the chance to cross the border, to examine the other side and size up our adversary.

When he returned, he didn't wait long. He had left behind in West Beirut a house destroyed by shells, bombed twice over. But with the Israelis pulling out of the capital, to remain in an occupied zone was out of the question. Besides, I was convinced, and rightly so, that the unexpected vigor of the resistance led by my comrades had forced the Israeli retreat.

My mother returned with my father to Beirut to examine the extent of the damage. After some hasty repairs, we were able to return to our home.

Back in West Beirut after those few months' absence, I was reunited with my neighborhood and my friends. Everything seemed the same, but things had deeply changed. The radio reports of the war were no longer only about our fratricidal, and hopelessly lost, guerrilla fighters. Now there was a place on the airwaves for reports of resistance operations against the Israelis. I began to feel, for the first time in the city I still called my own, the subtle control of the Lebanese Army over our lives. The Union of Democratic Youth was not banned, but we were clearly watched closely. We had to take this situation into account, although I found it to be ludicrous, absurd—in my eyes, the army was completely off the mark.

Two incidents marked my return. On November 22, Lebanese Independence Day, we decided to hold a demonstration protesting the Israeli presence. The Lebanese Army let us know that they did not favor this idea. Defying them, we put the youngest first in the march, children aged six to twelve. We were convinced that the soldiers would not dare take action against unarmed children. Of course, we were mistaken. The soldiers didn't hesitate to fire on the crowd, wounding many young people, who were rushed to the hospital. Shortly thereafter, a Lebanese teenager named Bilal Fahas carried out a suicide bombing against an Israeli vehicle. We decided to print up posters in his honor, and secretly pasted them all over the city. We went in pairs, one boy and one girl, and when a patrol came in sight we avoided their attention by pretending to be lovers.

During those dark years, devastating attacks were made on foreign troops deployed in Beirut, and French and American soldiers paid a high price for their countries' intervention. I resisted the idea of suicide bombings, just as I opposed the use of violence in general unless it was the only possible means of struggle. But I thought these acts were inevitable. These soldiers had come supposedly to restore peace, but weren't they just playing into the hands of the Israelis? They found themselves inevitably taking sides in a war that spared nothing and no one. My apprenticeship in politics sped up dramatically during 1982, that terrible year. The Israeli invasion gave me a bitter strength in my beliefs.

I was fifteen, and I was now ready to move into action.

6 COMMITMENT

A demonstration in Beirut for the disappeared, the kidnapped and confined.

The civil war, not satisfied with taking lives, stole people, too. For their families, there was nothing to do but wait. At noon on the day of the protest, cars were supposed to stop dead in the middle of the street as a sign of solidarity. My friends from the Union and I would ourselves block traffic on some of the main thoroughfares.

Our plan that day turned into a fiasco.

The traffic went about its way, undisturbed. One driver, totally indifferent, started up his car right in front of me. His attitude sent me into a white fury. Normally I was in perfect control of my emotions, but I suddenly lost my cool. I began to rail at him for his lack of feeling towards his fellow citizens. He was blasé, assuring me that all our efforts were totally useless and would come to nothing.

Another night, much later.

That night at midnight I heard of the death of Raghib Harb, one of the leaders of the resistance. He was a Shiite Muslim Shiekh from the little village of Jibshit, near Tyre, and he preached ceaselessly against the Israeli occupation. As both a religious figure and a member of Amal, he had a tremendous influence, igniting and tending the flame of resistance in countless villagers. He had just been killed, in his mosque, by the Israelis. The brutal slaying affected me deeply. As dawn broke, I ran to visit Ali, the Union head for West Beirut high school students. I woke him and told him the news. Together, we decided to organize a gathering in the school as a sign of mourning and a protest against Israel, followed by a procession through the streets.

I was the spokesperson for our school, so I was assigned to go to our principal and get the green light. I hurried to her office, where I was met with a refusal. She understood my feelings and my anger, but refused to cancel classes yet again. Our school life was already so disrupted by all the events stemming from the civil war. She was unyielding, and her attitude exasperated me. Beside myself with anger, I took her to task with all the righteousness of my fifteen years, giving her a lesson in patriotism. Somehow I managed to change her mind, and we found a compromise. In the morning we would study, then later we could have an assembly to explain what had just happened, then go to demonstrate in West Beirut. Ours was the only school to march through the streets that day. Usually the procession would begin at Sanaye Garden, then take the wide Hamra Street to the UN offices, then go along the Corniche, passing in front of the Kuwaiti Embassy. This time, we had to settle for a march around the neighborhood, without banners. I shouted slogans with so much energy that a man who saw me remarked to no one in particular: "That girl—she'll end up a suicide bomber, that's for sure!"

Altogether, it was a mediocre day.

Yet again, I had lost my cool. It had happened too often. It was high time to focus all that restless energy towards other ends.

Ever since the announcement, on September 16, 1982, of the creation of a united Lebanese Resistance Front against the Israeli occupation, my mind was made up. I was going to join them. But to do what? With whom? Under what conditions? I hardly had a clue. I felt a deep need to take part in the struggle which was just beginning, but when it came time to get in contact with the resistance I so idealized, I was at a total loss. The movement had been forced into secrecy in Beirut, which didn't help matters much. And I made a secret of my beliefs as well, even to my family and close friends. At the Union, we often wondered whether we too would be able to perform acts of daring. But I was careful to hide any glimmer of the flame that I'd been tending since that infamous September. I forced myself to act like a diligent student who stubbornly refused to go out at night, preferring to stay home and work. I pretended to be an active but moderate spokesperson. But, to risk sounding grandiloquent, sacrificing oneself for the cause no longer seemed like a taboo. In January 1985, Sanaa Mehaydle, eighteen years old, became the first girl to commit a suicide attack in the occupied zone, voluntarily detonating the bomb she carried in the middle of an Israeli patrol.

I was a pacifist at heart—but, struck by her example, I was ready to join the struggle.

My path required me to give up many things. This became quite clear after I turned fifteen, reaching that age when—both in school and in the Union—the camaraderie between boys and girls gave way to less disinterested feelings, even real passion. I had already been the object of the affections of one of my friends. He was a Party member who looked on the Union with some disdain, considering us immature and only just playing around. His was the first declaration of love I ever received, and I listened to him curiously. I didn't discourage his feelings, but after thinking it over for a few days, I felt that such a link would prevent me from fully pursuing my ideas. At that time, I was already offering to accompany different people in their cars when they drove around Beirut. I hardly needed to be asked—I knew that at the checkpoints a young couple attracted less attention than a single man. And those cars could possibly be used to carry weapons.

So there were consequences to any serious commitment to the struggle. Besides, I had plenty of examples around me that advised me not to confuse my personal feelings with the resistance.

In my search for the resistance network, I became close to a girl comrade whose boyfriend was active in a Marxist group. I knew he was liable to be involved in armed struggle. My friend wanted to join him, to fight by his side, but he said it was too dangerous for her—he didn't want to expose her to any risk, no matter how slight. Because of this, they eventually separated.

Another friend of mine suffered the same dilemma. This time, her boyfriend was fighting with Hezbollah. He became observant to such a degree that my friend was quite put off, and she decided to break up with him. Just at that point, she learned that he was about to participate in a suicide attack. She was sure that she was partly responsible for his choice, and she asked me to come south with her to try and talk him out of going through with it. For me, this was a stroke of luck—it meant making contact with the resistance movement. I agreed, and we were on our way. My friend eventually managed to change her boyfriend's mind. Truth be told, he had done everything he could to encourage her, by letting her know of his plans and then giving her a way to find him. I understood my friend's feelings and actions, even if, at bottom, I somewhat disapproved of her.

I realized from what I saw around me that people could choose to commit themselves to the struggle, even sacrifice their lives, for personal reasons that often had little to do with patriotism. My cousin Loula, a Communist, was another of these thwarted lovers. She died during a mission in the Bekaa Valley, having broken up with her boyfriend just a short time earlier.

These examples came as a relief to me. Each time, I was sure that I had made the right choice in avoiding all entanglements, even with my comrades of the resistance. Of course, like all girls my age, I dreamed of having a lover, of sharing a life with common projects, of having a family and children of my own. But it seemed impossible to me, under the circumstances, to lead a double life. From then on, my relationships with boys were limited to friendship. For them, I even became a sort of confidante, a social and emotional helper. My girlfriends would also ask my advice on intimate matters. They thought that I was more up-to-date on such issues because of my closeness to the Communist Party, which was considered to be an emancipatory force.

In fact, I suffered little from my decision to not have a boyfriend. I dreamed of one thing, and one thing only: joining the resistance.

Achieving this ambition was not easy. I took an active part in the movement against the humiliating agreement of May 17, 1983, signed between Israel and Amin Gemayel, the leader of its Lebanese allies. Our movement was effective, and the agreement was later broken. At that time, my whole family wanted to get me out of the country. My mother feared that I would commit the worst act she thought possible for a young Orthodox Lebanese girl—that I would marry a Muslim. My father hoped that I would follow the model of my brother Adnan and study abroad, far from the civil war and its ever-increasing scenes of violence and horror. I had a feeling that one of my sister's teachers might put me on the trail of the resistance, but I was sure that if I breathed a word to him, he would immediately warn my parents. To cap it all off, my first efforts to broach the subject with him were met with a flat refusal. I finally made up my mind to ask Ali. He was the political figure I most trusted, and I could count on his silence. But he retorted that my use to the movement was with the Union and in my school. For him, my future lay along those lines. This meant that I was elected, practically kicking and screaming in protest, to the Union's National Council. My name was printed in the newspapers—not a good start for someone hoping to go into clandestine action. I forced myself to fade into the background in the student movement, ostensibly in the name of my all-important studies.

Out of ideas, I thought of abandoning the engineering school in which—to the great joy of my parents—I had just enrolled. I would leave my family and Beirut and move to the South. I thought that by getting married and settling down there, I would be bound to quietly find some sort of solution. One day I told Ali of my decision to leave for the occupied zone, just a word in passing.

Suddenly, my lost hopes materialized.

My persistence had probably won him over. He answered by telling me that "a certain person" wanted to meet me, and that a rendezvous would soon be arranged. When I got home, I put on some music and danced wildly around the room.

Finally, I had found my contact!

On the day of the meeting, I cautiously made my way to an apartment in West Beirut. Ali came with me. He introduced me to a man in his forties who called himself "M.A." He was tall and good-looking, with light skin and fair hair. He was discreet, nearly uncommunicative. His words betrayed no hint of his social or religious origin. We spoke of one thing and another, and then Ali slipped away, leaving "M.A." and me alone. We began to talk about the situation in Lebanon, the civil war and the resistance. I told him that I felt it was my duty to take part. If we did nothing, I said, we Lebanese would suffer the same fate as the Palestinians. I told him that I was determined to do whatever it took, that I was willing to go all the way. M.A. let me talk, trying to cool my fire by telling me that people quite naturally back down in the face of danger. I remained steadfast in my determination.

Two more meetings soon followed. M.A. inquired about my reading. My answer was simple. A Communist admirer had given me a book in 1983 which recounted some feat of the Red Army against the Germans during the Second World War. Apart from this, I had basically read nothing outside of my schoolwork—no newspapers, no books of history or politics. M.A. began by giving me a pamphlet with the explicit title of *Viet Cong*. The little 50-page book was written in Arabic and had been printed in Beirut. He then offered me a selection of many other books. I chose *The Dialectics of History*, a huge 1200-page tome in Arabic which my new mentor had specially arranged to borrow from a Russian bookstore. I only had time to read about a hundred pages. I couldn't take it with me on my missions to the South, nor could I leave it at home.

Our topics of discussion became more and more concrete. M.A. was looking specifically for Christians to send on missions to the South. They were less likely to arouse suspicion on the part of the pro-Israeli militias, who, with the IDF, controlled the occupied zone. He advised me not to change any of my habits, above all to continue living with my family, and to pursue my studies with my usual dedication. He explained that everyone should be rooted in a family. The resistance was working to liberate the whole Lebanese people.

In March 1986, after taking my exams, I went to stay with an aunt in the South. It was my first test, although strictly speaking I didn't have any particular mission to fulfill.

When I returned to Beirut, I found disaster.

I went back to our usual spot, but M.A. was not there. He had disappeared, leaving me no hint of what might have happened. For three months I had no news of him. I was in despair. I had held my dream in my hands, but that dream had suddenly vanished. It was no use talking to Ali. I had to wait. Later, I found out that M.A. had been kidnapped by Amal—kidnapped and tortured. During those months, I wandered about like a lost soul. I couldn't concentrate on my schoolwork, and I failed my exams for the first time ever. Finally, after many long weeks, a glimmer of hope—M.A. had left a message for me at Union headquarters.

Once again, I had picked up the thread.

When I met M.A. a few days later, he told me nothing of his trials. He just mentioned that he had not revealed any information about me. We took up our conversations where we had left off. At first I thought that joining the resistance would be quick and easy—that I would be given an explosive and a target, and that the rest would be understood. But I learned that an operation was much more sophisticated than that. It required careful preparation, close study of the terrain, and attention to countless details. When I told M.A. about my time in the South, he asked me to write a report, three 8 1/2" by 11" sheets, where I was to set down all I had seen.

At around the same time, I invented a plausible excuse, for my friends and family, to justify my travel to and from the South. His name was Sohad. He was a lab technician at the hospital in Marjayoun, the little town where my cousin Issam also worked, managing a private clinic with his wife. Sohad was around twenty-six and had a good job, and he was quite good-looking.

I planted this information among my friends, and it spread like wildfire. I took care to confide my secret only with the worst gossips. While I was out walking one night with my sister, she asked me if this boy was really worth so much traveling. I managed to work myself into a rage, and almost brutally told her to worry about her own love story, which was a real one, with our complicated neighbor Pierre.

After that night, everyone understood that I was not to be bothered about what I was doing in the South.

One day, M.A. told me that we would be meeting for the last time, and that from then on another member of the organization would take care of me. We were to meet in a café. I was to buy the women's magazine *al-Hasna* and seem to be absorbed in it. We had a security code: if I thought I was being watched or followed, I would set a pack of Marlboros on the table in a special way to give the alert. That day, a man calling himself Rabih was to come and meet me. After many detours through the city, I eventually made my way to the café. From my very first meeting with M.A., I developed the habit of passing time in shops, particularly those with mirrors. There, I could take precautions, and discreetly check if someone was trailing me. I made contact with Rabih as planned. I had passed to another level. Now I was in contact with the active branch of the resistance.

Our meetings became more frequent. It was June of 1986; as of September, after the holidays, I would be spending more and more time in the occupied zone.

I was about to be given a new clandestine mission.

7 PREPARATIONS

In just a few years, the occupation had transformed South Lebanon.

Traditions and whole ways of life had been turned upside-down. Since Lebanese began to work in Israel, the holidays had changed. Weddings were now held on Saturdays, the obligatory Sabbath, rather than on Sundays as before. And money, even more than the presence of Israeli troops, helped to destabilize social relations. By working for the Israelis or the occupying army, young women earned much more than what was offered in Beirut. They were heavily courted, not for themselves, but for their spending power. Marriages became less stable and divorces increased.

South Lebanon was a classic lawless zone, open to any kind of traffic. At the dinner table, bottles of *arak* were replaced by bottles of Johnny Walker. Drugs in transit, cars stolen in Europe—any type of product could be found there. For those who had problems with the law in their native country, South Lebanon became an ideal refuge, especially since the South Lebanese Army, run by Antoine Lahad, had few scruples about who they would hire.

This was the strange world I discovered on my first visit, shortly after making contact with M.A. in Beirut. I was reunited with friends and relatives, and I tried hard to blend into my surroundings, hoping to learn as much as possible. Of course, mentioning the resistance directly was out of the question. The subject was completely taboo. Security forces were everywhere, either linked to the SLA or directly controlled by Shin Bet, the Israeli internal security agency.

I couldn't have said that the Lebanese I met there were particularly pro-Israeli. In fact, they were all very attached to their country, and to their families, who were often settled on either side of the demarcation line. People even tried their best, when they had enough money, to buy a pied-a-terre in Beirut. But above all, they tried to profit as much as possible from their situation. Buffeted by history and by the fortunes of war, faced with a society knocked off balance, they worked to make the most of it. Each looked after his own interests, not worrying about how much compromise or collaboration with the occupying powers this really meant. No one thought the situation could last. But at the same time, people found it difficult to imagine that, some day, Israel might pull back inside its borders. The ridiculous Lebanese phantom state, with its army, its military, and political leaders, clouded people's vision. Why couldn't South Lebanon separate from Lebanon, becoming a kind of buffer state between Israel and its Arab neighbors to the north? The SLA soldiers, who had served in the Lebanese Army before becoming Israeli auxiliaries, thought that even if Lebanon were to regain its sovereignty over this conquered region, they would be able to return to their old jobs via an amnesty. No choice seemed to be past recall.

As the daughter of a notorious Communist militant, and having grown up in a leftist village known for being critical of the government, I had to be careful to avoid suspicion. At this point in my service, I had no specific mission. I was just expected to report back to Beirut, to increase my contacts with South Lebanese and, if possible, with members of the security services in the occupied zone. I did everything to look like a sociable young girl: athletic, happy, totally uninterested in the political and military issues at stake in the occupied zone. I juggled the requirements for permission to go to and from the zone, applying alternately in Beirut and in the South, covering my tracks by asking both the SLA and the Israelis. I traveled sometimes through West Beirut and sometimes through the East. Eventually, I officially began to look for a job in the South. In the capital, I still used my supposed love affair as an alibi. To any observer in the occupied zone, I was just looking to profit from all the riches diverted to flow through the controlled region.

During the time when I had lost contact with M.A., I had asked myself if I was ready to have a relationship with an Israeli, in order to draw him into a trap. With a Lebanese friend, I even forced myself into a kind of "exercise in seduction" to see if I was able to go that far. In the end, the result was pitiful. Put to the test, I couldn't cross the line. I had gone back to his place ready for anything, but face to face in the intimacy of his room I couldn't do it. My unlucky friend must have wondered what came over me that day, especially since as a militant Communist I had the reputation of being a liberated woman, making me an ideal partner for free and easy amorous exchange.

I learned from Rabih the basics of gathering information. You had to be able to identify troop movements, evaluate their strength, note down the unit numbers, and draw their positions. It was also important to protect yourself, to use the utmost caution in contacting the resistance, and to work with total discretion. I thought I would be quickly trained and then go marching out to war. Instead I learned patience, and the need to return again and again to the South in order to understand the workings of the SLA.

I had one temporary disagreement with my mentor. An Israeli office had been quietly set up in Ashrafiya, in East Beirut. He suggested I take a look at it. I could guess what he was getting at—organizing a bombing—but I was not interested in any kind of operation in Beirut. I managed to win my case.

For me, the war had to be carried out in the occupied zone.

Starting in July 1987, my trips to the South became part of a specific mission. I had been given three targets: the men of the SLA security forces, the Israelis, and Antoine Lahad himself. At that time, the idea of South Lebanon's secession was very much in vogue. Targeting its supposed leader seemed like the best way to ruin Israel's plans. Israel had already pushed Antoine Lahad's predecessor, Saad Haddad, into declaring the parcel of land he controlled to be a "Free State." I was supposed to work on the ground to find out which target would be easiest to hit. To this end, I maintained all kinds of contacts, and accepted invitations to various parties and ceremonies. I became progressively closer to the security forces in the village of Hasbaya, near Marjayoun. I don't think anybody I talked to was fooled by my attitude. Was I just ambitious, or was it something else? Underneath the pat phrases laden with politeness and civility, everyone watched each other, sized each other up. Weeks passed. I saw no clear way forward. I split my time between Deir Mimas, staying with my aunt since my aging grandparents had joined their children in Beirut, and Marjayoun, at my cousin Issam's.

Issam was married, and he tried to shelter his two children from the strange events that spun around them. He had good relations with most of the local militiamen and with the Israelis, but his attitude was more complex than it seemed. In order to preserve his interests, he worked to win the Israelis' trust. But deep down, as a dyed-in-the-wool Communist, he was opposed to the occupation. His wife, Jeannette, had even once been tempted to join the resistance. He knew my family's— especially my father's—reputation, and so on my arrival he tried to sound out my intentions and beliefs. One day, during a car trip, we passed by a well-known spot where some members of the resistance had orchestrated a devastating attack. He asked me offhandedly what I thought about that kind of behavior. Naturally, I took care not to give away my real thoughts. On the contrary—I said that I couldn't understand or accept such violence, and made a plea for mutual goodwill and understanding. My cousin seemed quite satisfied with this answer.

After that, he treated me like a somewhat naive girl, plainly out of touch with the political realities of the day.

As of June 1988, I settled full-time in the South. Once there, it was hard to keep in touch with Beirut. Already, in 1987, I had been given fifteen days advance notice of an Israeli military offensive on Kfar Tibnit, a village bordering the occupied zone, but I was unable to pass the message along.

When I returned to Beirut, I was advised to work in contact with the resistance network in the South. I refused, knowing that I was probably under surveillance. We worked out another solution: the exchange of coded messages by telephone. A little while later, I had some information to verify. A party was supposedly being planned. It was to feature a recital by a famous Lebanese singer, and Antoine Lahad and some Israeli officials might attend—a good chance for a military operation. But nothing on the ground confirmed the news. Planning anything was pointless. I went to the telephone exchange and called a friend in Beirut, telling him to "keep my chemistry and physics textbooks with my notes." He knew what I was talking about.

During our last few meetings, Rabih had given me only one piece of advice: to keep my distance from the Hasbaya security services, whom he mistrusted. I could not accept this. Though I was focusing my efforts on Marjayoun, where Antoine Lahad lived, I felt that I couldn't stop going to visit the people I knew in Hasbaya, even if it were just to muddy my tracks. I decided to find a job in a strategic place. The idea of working as an operator in the telephone exchange appealed to me, and I asked Issam to recommend me to the manager. Hadn't he already made me an offer one day, in Issam's presence? But when I asked Issam, he cried out in protest. I had to admit that the people working at the exchange did not have the best reputation, to say the least. They were completely tied up with the security services, and, according to Issam, their morals were quite suspect.

"Unbelievable! You just don't get it. You're too naive," cried my cousin, truly indignant. I replied that I absolutely needed to find work, and I offered to help out at the Marjayoun sports and cultural center. Since I had a taste for this kind of activity, the idea made sense, and it quickly calmed Issam down. He eventually gave his full approval, assuring me that he himself would put me in touch with the director.

We made an appointment. Issam came with me to the center. The interview went off without a hitch. The director was sympathetic, and I had no trouble convincing him of my passion for sports. I offered to give ping-pong and gymnastics classes. He was delighted. He even went beyond my wildest dreams by telling me, there and then, that, as it happened, the leader of the SLA's wife was looking for an aerobics instructor. I quickly saw my opening. I assured him, peppering my words with impressive French expressions, that I happened to be quite familiar with this kind of training.

The wife of the head of the army in the occupied zone! That kind of position couldn't be easy. Minerva Lahad was said to be an attractive and energetic young woman from the chic Beirut suburb of Ashrafiya. She was bored, more often than not, by this artificial universe supported by Israeli generosity. There, everyone knew and watched one another, each vying with the other in gossip and unkind words, and she was not spared. At one time I had thought of going more often to the Marjayoun hairdresser, hoping to meet her—she was always there. But my personality didn't fit with that kind of a project, and my behavior would have been suspicious. Although I had made progress in terms of fashion since I had come to the South, no longer wearing my usual Beirut outfit of T-shirt and jeans, I still resisted styling my hair or using make-up. On the other hand, the idea of giving aerobics lessons was a perfect fit.

An interview with Minerva Lahad was arranged. Issam went with me to her house, helping me pass quickly through the security checkpoints where I was searched only lightly. The house had been requisitioned by Antoine Lahad, himself originally from the Bekaa valley. It was spacious and well furnished. Minerva, who was indeed very pretty and much younger than her husband, made a good impression on me. She was intelligent and cultivated, and had obviously been well educated. She spoke to her children only in French. She struggled to live up to the somewhat ridiculous title that history had provided for her: First Lady of South Lebanon. At the same time, I felt that she had difficulties gaining the acceptance of Marjayoun society. Minerva described her problem to me. She was presently under the thumb of a dance teacher who was continually squeezing money out of her students, making outrageous profits from the situation. She hurried to trot out a list of nearly thirty candidates for that voluntary torture called aerobics. If I gave an acceptable demonstration of my talents, they could all be my students. I would be judged by a friend of Minerva's, the French wife of a Lebanese doctor. I said I was delighted by the opportunity, and that I would be ready to start giving lessons as soon as I had time away from university in Beirut, which would be very soon. Actually, I was eager to tell my superiors what had happened, and I wanted to minimize the risk by going to Beirut myself.

I was quite content. Finally, a stroke of luck, a real opening. I was on the verge of placing myself at the heart of the SLA, a unique vantage point for gleaning maximum information on the habits and movements of the army's leader. From the beginning of our talks, Rabih and I had raised the possibility of an attack against Antoine Lahad, and now it seemed to be taking shape.

When I met Rabih a few days later, I was proud of what I had achieved, and my superior was enthusiastic. But at that point neither of us knew what might be targeted, nor by whom. While visiting Beirut, I got a friend of mine to make copies of some of Jane Fonda's workout tapes. I asked my sister, a fitness instructor, a few innocent questions, and then headed for Marjayoun to get ready for the big test. I took advantage of the absence of Issam and his wife to replay the tapes on their VCR. The illusion had to be complete. I fine-tuned a kind of ballet, stringing together various exercises to a soundtrack of pounding music.

Two days after my return, I passed the most important test of my life.

My classes got off to a rough start, but I made the most of it. I had to return several times to Antoine Lahad's house to work out all the details. We quickly agreed on a salary. I had to make a plausible request, not too high and not too low, since I had supposedly come South to find work. With thirty students, five dollars per student seemed reasonable. All we had to do was find them. When we met for the first time, Minerva had assured me that, considering the lack of activities in the occupied zone, we wouldn't need to do any publicity. All her friends had encouraged her to find an instructor. But we soon had to change our tune. The other women did not follow through on their promises, and it threw Minerva into a rage. She was obviously being mocked—they were dead set on keeping her isolated.

Far from being discouraged, she plunged into the search. It took on an unexpected importance; she simply refused to let it go. Antoine Lahad, when asked, offered his unconditional support. The lessons started with a small group, only five students, but nevertheless, they started. There was still the question of money. With so few students, I was far from my hoped-for pay.

Minerva turned to her husband to solve this delicate question, and so I met him for the first time.

Rabih had already shown me a photo of the former Lebanese Army Officer, but he looked quite different than I remembered. In just a few years, his features had greatly altered. He did not seem particularly unlikeable. He worked hard to humor his wife. He even offered to fill the gap in my salary out of his own pocket. I accepted, telling him how devoted I was to this project.

After I said goodbye, a decision slowly began to ripen in my mind. From then on, I would be there, in place, near our target. So it was up to me to do it, to perform the most ambitious mission that we could then imagine —to kill Antoine Lahad.

8 THE OPERATION

I met again with my contact at the heart of the resistance.

Rabih listened as I told him about my first interview with Antoine Lahad. Right away, he made it clear that we would have to plan for me to be replaced by someone whose job it would be to eliminate the militia chief. I answered that, considering the circumstances, I myself was in the best position to succeed. Rabih was not very taken with this idea. He admitted its efficiency, but he seriously doubted that I was capable of carrying out the operation. But faced with my stubbornness, he resigned himself to taking the risk. There was still the question of the weapon. Once again, Rabih advised me to make contact with the resistance in the South; they would be able to get me something. I refused. I felt like I was constantly being followed, even in Beirut, where I had to invent all kinds of diversions. When I was supposed to make contact with my superiors and thought that someone was tailing me, I would simply give up, not even trying to shake my guardian angels. Even if I was in the clear, I still had the habit of going by a friend's place, where as a precaution I could change clothes and slip out via the terrace.

Time was short, so Rabih and I decided to meet in a discreet spot, a café where couples often went on dates. That day, he secretly brought with him a 5.5 mm revolver. In a few words he told me how it worked, pointing out the safety catch. On my return trip, I had no difficulties. I passed through the checkpoints without a worry, the gun taped right to my skin. Issam had come to Beirut to pick me up, and I knew that, thanks to him and his contacts, I would not be searched. Once I reached home, I hid the gun under my mattress, then stuck it inside an old television set that was sitting around my room.

I took my role of aerobics instructor very seriously. Little by little, I became quite close to Minerva. She adored the very feminine clothes my mother made for me, which I now wore much more often. She even asked me if my dressmaker wouldn't mind making something for her. I managed to avoid the question. Otherwise, our classes became quite successful. The militia chief's wife was enthusiastic, and imagined organizing a competition with the Israelis that could then be shown on Israeli television. So I found myself going again and again to her house, either to bring her videocassettes or to work out problems with the classes. When she was busy or indisposed and I had to wait, I would play with her little son, whose affection I easily gained.

Step by step, I fine-tuned my plan, but still I felt all sorts of dangers rising around me. In Beirut, my friends who knew that I had settled in the South became ill at ease in my presence. A Christian going back and forth between Beirut and the occupied zone was suspicious, to say the least. It didn't help that a video was making the rounds in Hasbaya showing me dancing at a party in the company of Israelis and militiamen. There were no secrets in Lebanon. My friends didn't want me to become a collaborator or spy. One of them came to see me, trying to protect me. He warned me in a general way against the irresistible lure of money, the lifeblood of the occupied zone. Others close to me thought that I was living in East Beirut, thanks to my mother, who put about the rumor to help me avoid an even worse reputation. The rumor convinced my cousin Emile, who solemnly urged me not to socialize with the Israeli-allied Phalangists, if only in memory of our cousin Loula. I struggled to reassure him, telling him that it was not at all what I had in mind.

Amal also became interested in me. I was given a message telling me I would not be allowed to go into the area of Beirut where Amal's leader, Nabih Berri, lived. In Nabatiya one day, I just barely escaped a search party of members of that movement, who had been sent to find me.

In the occupied zone, too, the questioning became more frequent. In Marjayoun, Antoine Lahad and his entourage tried to learn more about me. I felt a subtle pressure that revealed itself in little things. The way I was shadowed when I left for Deir Mimas and then returned to Issam's. The subtle grilling I received when I traveled to Hasbaya accompanied by members of the security forces. That day, I was supposed to go with Minerva to find a battery for the tape player I used in my classes. But in the end, it was the "heavies" who escorted me. In the car, I was casually questioned about my family and my ideas. I was now an old hand at this exercise, and I chattered away, giving the impression that I had nothing to hide.

I had the feeling, all told, that Antoine Lahad was not quite fooled by my role of aerobics instructor. Put on guard by his entourage, he probably thought me a little spy sent to gather as much information about him as possible. I don't think, however, that in his eyes I represented the type of fighter ready to do anything for the cause. I was also lucky enough to take advantage of the rivalry between the Hasbaya security forces and the SLA military leaders in Marjayoun. The first were mostly Druze and Shiite Muslim, the second mostly Christian. The Hasbaya security forces, who probably had more precise information about me, treated me with the most suspicion.

Ever since I was given a weapon, I decided to carry it with me whenever I went to the Lahad house. It was a considerable risk. I was at the mercy of one of the SLA leader's personal bodyguards, who was more conscientious than his colleagues and took it upon himself to search me. Once, then twice, I managed to make it into the house with the revolver hidden in my purse.

One day, the unthinkable occurred.

I was talking with Minerva when her husband suddenly came home. He joined us, and we talked a moment about the classes. His wife offered to fix him something to eat. Obviously hungry, he accepted with pleasure.

Minerva excused herself, leaving me alone with her husband. We continued our conversation. She came back with the food, then left again. The head of the militia turned away from me and attacked his meal. Startled, I didn't know what to do. It was the perfect opportunity. I was armed. His back was turned. I plunged my hand into the purse I carried by my side and pulled out...a handkerchief. I could feel the heavy weight of the revolver against my hip, but something stopped me from grabbing it. Not like that. Not so summary, in the middle of a meal. Not in the back.

I couldn't kill my enemy under those conditions.

I left the house a few moments later, deeply confused, having taken leave of my host, who seemed to suspect nothing. I was as determined as ever, but for the first time I realized the difficulty of the task, the self-will that murder, however justified it was in my eyes, implied. In that summer of 1988, after thirteen years of civil war and all kinds of horror, I realized that I was still just as resistant to brutality and force, still just as disturbed by violence, even the fictional violence shown on television. The car bombings, the wounded whom I had treated, the memories of the dead, none of it had hardened me.

And I knew that I would have to overcome this repulsion.

That September, like every other, my mother traveled to Deir Mimas to lay in provisions for the winter. She did not know it yet, but it would be one of her last trips to the village. In Beirut, she had been shaken by a warning given by my uncle Nayef. He was sure that I was in the South on a mission. Based on his personal experience in the Party, which he had by then left, he suspected something. He ordered his sister-in-law to forbid me from returning to Deir Mimas or Marjayoun.

But my mother's fears vanished when she arrived in the village. Nearly everyone sang her daughter's praises, painting a portrait of me as spontaneous, energetic, and sweet. My mother was quite pleased and flattered. On top of this, a lucky chance led my supposed lover to drop by our house. The young man, so good-looking, wanted to invite me to a party. For my mother, it was a real soap opera. She even wrote me a few days later inviting me to come and help her with the olive harvest!

Having set her mind at rest, I took off for Beirut, to meet with

Rabih once again. Officially, I was leaving the occupied zone to take my exams, which were indeed to be held on the date I had mentioned. At Rabih's office in Saida, I skimmed mechanically over my study notes while waiting for him to free himself up. When he came out, he was stupefied to see me so hard at work. Studying for an exam just a few days before a possible operation, working at classes that I would probably never continue, seemed to him totally absurd. Once his surprise had passed, he led me into the presence of other leaders of the resistance.

Once again, the question was asked: was I fully prepared, psychologically, for such an act? My mind was made up, and I pleaded my case—successfully. Once the idea of a bomb attack had been put aside, we looked at the possibility of using poisoned bullets, to help put the odds in our favor. Rabih knew my aversion to violence, and he guessed that a revolver like the 5.5 mm, which has a highly destructive impact, did not suit me. But a smaller caliber gun would do the trick.

After deciding on the weapon, we left for the isolation of a piece of waste ground, where I could practice a few training shots. We knew that time was short, and that our project had to be finished quickly. I explained my vision of the thing to Rabih. I would not shoot him in the head, as Rabih had advised me, nor would I empty the chamber of bullets into my enemy's body. I told Rabih what I had decided ever since I had begun to imagine it seriously. Two bullets in the direction of his heart would be enough.

My last few days in Beirut passed in a flash.

I tried to make it so that my words betrayed no emotion, no outburst of fear. I chatted with my friends about a cake I was baking for an upcoming party. I talked with my sister about love, and readied myself to part from my father, telling him nothing. With Rabih, I spent one of my last free nights. He gave me advice and support, and asked me to write a letter explaining my act. I wrote about the civil war, the Israeli invasion, and the death of our heroes. I expressed my admiration for the Palestinian intifada, which had just broken out in the Occupied Territories, and which seemed to me to be a beauti-

ful example of resistance and an ideal of revolution. My last
night at home, I burnt in secret my favorite photos of myself,
fearing that they would be used by the Party for propaganda
about the "martyrs" of the resistance. But I still gave a few snap-
shots to Rabih. This side of things exasperated me, and when
Rabih told me the *nom de guerre* that the Party had chosen for
me—"Flower of the South"—I rudely cut him short.

On the morning of my departure, I said goodbye to my
father, not knowing if I would see him again one day.

I had no idea what awaited me. I suspected it was quite likely that things would go badly for me, but whether the operation succeeded or failed, I couldn't conceive that my whole
existence might just end. As agreed, I went to the university for
my exams. I slipped out before the end. Rabih was waiting outside. He had promised to accompany me to the northern limit
of the occupied zone. We were soon on our way. The trip was
short, but Rabih seemed extremely tense. He was worried that
the weapon I carried would be discovered at the checkpoint.
On our arrival, after a last brief conversation, we said goodbye.

At the checkpoint, the militiawoman who had the job of
searching women was not there. I had no authorization to pass.
A soldier got ready to take her place. I did not know him. His
hands lingered on me. I felt him unintentionally touch the
revolver I wore under my clothes, fixed with care by Rabih. The
soldier, his mind obviously on other things, did not react. I
interrupted his search, asking quite naturally to see his boss,
"Monsieur Raymond," who I said was expecting me. The soldier, impressed, left off his eager palpitations, and let me pass
without going through the metal detector. His superior was
there, but I had no problem slipping away after a short chat
with his subordinates.

Back in the occupied South, the atmosphere was even more
tense than on my previous visit. For some time, the Hasbaya
security services had been trying to convince me to work with
them. I was the ideal recruit: a Christian living in West Beirut
who had freedom of movement. I also imagined that signing

up with them would help dispel the doubts that they had about me and my activities.

When I got to Marjayoun, I learned that the head of security, Alam al-Dine, wanted to see me. It wasn't the first time that I was so directly approached. The previous July, I had met the man in the Hasbaya barracks. He was slightly drunk, railing against "those terrorists who murder SLA men." A wad of American dollars lay casually on his desk. He tried to intimidate me, and draw information out of me, without success. He then proposed that I carry messages out of the occupied zone. With him, I decided not to hide my family's involvement with the Communist Party. I didn't say much, just talked about how I liked that the Party was open to people of any religious background. I added that I wasn't really interested in politics, and we left it at that.

I began to notice that the security services were no longer happy about my coming and going through different checkpoints. They struggled to centralize my movements. Issam, noticing that I was visibly worried, asked me what was going on. I tried to explain to him that, as an independent-minded person, I couldn't bear being so scrutinized, and that I owed the Hasbaya people nothing. Issam's wife, Jeannette, supported me in my protest. Without telling me, Issam decided to intervene on my behalf. One night, during a wedding in Deir Mimas, he blocked one of Alam al-Dine's deputies—a man named Kamil who seemed quite interested in me—from giving me any trouble.

The weeks passed, and the tension stayed high. I kept up with my aerobics classes, waiting for my chance to visit the house of Antoine Lahad.

One Sunday in November, at five o'clock in the morning, the security forces showed up at our house in Deir Mimas. They were looking for me. By chance, I had just left a few minutes earlier to harvest olives. Faced with my mother, they mumbled some vague pretext and left empty-handed, without revealing their real intentions. Later in the day, my mother worriedly told me about that unexpected early-morning visit.

Back in Marjayoun that same night, I realized that my room

had been searched. I always left a piece of clothing hanging in a special way in my closet, so I would notice any surprise incursions. When I returned to my den, I immediately saw that it had been moved. The security forces, yet again. Luckily, they had not found my guns. I had hidden the second revolver at the back end of a very long and heavy drawer. As I suspected, they had not opened it all the way.

However, the message was clear. I was in their sights. It was a question of days at the most. I knew that, given their rivalry, the security forces had certainly not asked Antoine Lahad for a green light before coming to see us that morning. There were no secrets in the occupied zone, and I figured they would wait a few days before their next move. I was sure, more than ever, that an arrest—or even a routine questioning—would break the bonds of trust that I had tried to build with Minerva Lahad.

I didn't have much time now.

It was hard to create the moment. A few days earlier I had gone back to Lahad's house, but he was in his office, meeting with an Israeli general. But the countdown had begun. One last time, I called Minerva to tell her that I had to return to Beirut, again because of my exams. I proposed to go by her place the next day, Monday, to leave her the keys for the exercise room, as well as the workout tapes she had asked for.

She agreed.

Wearing a white shirt, blue pants, and black ballet slippers, I made it once again without difficulty into the couple's beautiful house. I had been dropped off by Issam, who, to kill time, liked to join the nightly cavalcade of cars that filled the streets of Marjayoun. Before leaving, I had taken the revolver from its cache and hid it among a few other little things in my purse. The SLA chief's bodyguards let me pass without suspicion.

The usual routine.

I found Minerva in the garden with a Spanish friend. We moved inside, where we met her friend's husband, César, the director of a television station. Later, Antoine Lahad joined us. The atmosphere was pleasant. We spoke in French. Minerva lamented once again the small-mindedness of people in the occupied zone. We moved into the living room. The militia chief sat down near the telephone, with me to his right, as I had imagined. The conversation idled along. I kept myself a bit behind it all.

I listened.

After a half-hour, our hostess asked us what we'd like to drink. I murmured my thanks, but said that it was late and I had to go. Her husband insisted, and I made as if I was staying out of politeness. The militia chief turned on the television. It was the nightly news, on the station of the occupied zone. There was a report on the Intifada. On the screen, I had time to see a young Palestinian throwing a stone. Antoine Lahad watched distractedly, playing with the remote control. Suddenly, the telephone rang. He picked it up. His face darkened. Whoever he was talking to was obviously bringing up an unpleasant subject.

I stole a glance at the living room clock.

It was nearly eight. Sitting to my left, Antoine Lahad continued his conversation. His gaze rested on me for a moment. He examined me, as if curious. I drew towards me the bag lying at my feet. I was extraordinarily calm. I slid my hand into the opening, telling Minerva that I had brought the keys and videotapes she wanted. My hand, hidden from sight, closed on the handle of the gun. Still sitting, I took the weapon from the bag like it was the most natural thing in the world. Instantly, I pointed it towards the militia chief, supporting my fist with my left hand.

I struggled to aim at the condemned man's heart.

I pulled the trigger once and thought I saw the bullet bury itself in his khaki shirt. Antoine Lahad, taken aback, shot to his feet, as Rabih had predicted. An insult sprang from his lips: "Bitch!" I fired a second time, as planned.

He staggered.

For a second, life in the living room froze. Minerva, lying on the ground, let out a scream, shattering the silence. She cried for a gun to settle me and a helicopter to evacuate her husband. I threw a sweeping glance around me. The Spanish woman, her face ashen, looked at me fixedly, like a mad-woman. Her husband, paralyzed with terror, was staring at me like he would be next. I took the chance to throw the gun into the bedroom off the living room, trying to gain a little time. The bodyguards would look for the weapon as soon as they burst into the room, which would be soon enough. Six feet away from me, the militiaman's body had rolled to the floor and lay there, motionless.

9 THE ARREST

It was done. I had completed my mission.

What would happen to me now?

I had asked myself the question a thousand times since deciding to carry out the operation, and I had never found an answer. We had made no plans for me to escape, or for someone to rescue me. It would have been too dangerous. Antoine Lahad's house was like a fortified camp. I had been able to enter an hour earlier, fooling the guards one last time, then fire on the leader of Israel's proxy militia. But now the two shots had sounded the alert.

Inevitably, I would be arrested. But what would they do with me? Torture me? Execute me on the spot?

When I talked with Rabih for the last time before coming to the South, we had wondered about my fate in case of arrest. I thought that I would be imprisoned in the occupied zone, a territory outside the law where they could lock you up for years without any official trial. Rabih, for his part, was sure that if I managed to kill Antoine Lahad, the head of the SLA, I would most likely be thrown in an Israeli prison. But this seemed improbable to me, as the Geneva Convention forbids an occupying power from transferring detainees from one country to another.

During our conversation, I also raised the possibility that I might be tortured. "You can say whatever you like," he assured me. In fact, I didn't know much. I had no idea of Rabih's real name, and I was not in touch with the resistance network in the South. His only advice was not to mention the other hypotheses we had raised: kidnapping an Israeli, performing an operation against the security forces, or making off with Antoine Lahad's young son—an option that from the beginning I had rejected out of hand, even before I became close to the little boy.

I was still seated when César, the Spanish woman's husband, burst into the room. He took in the situation in a flash, sprang towards me, and put his hands on my shoulders.

"Why did you do it? Why did you kill him?" he asked me in French.

"He's the one killing us."

"Who sent you?"

"I work with the Lebanese Resistance. I belong to the Communist Party."

Minerva was trying to get at me, but César brushed her aside and she rushed to the telephone to call for help. A soldier came in. I recognized him. His name was Ibrahim. He dragged me from the armchair and locked me in his grip, moving me towards the door. When we got there, we stopped. "Don't shoot!" he cried. "It's me, don't shoot!"

As we stepped out the door we crossed paths with a neighbor of the Lahads, a Lebanese shopkeeper, who had rushed there with Ibrahim after hearing the shots. I knew him, too. He was a child-hood friend of mine, Lameh, also from Deir Mimas. His father had been head jailer at Khiam. Lameh gaped open-mouthed at me. I was just as surprised to see him. Then, overwhelmed, he put his head in his hands, and I went on without a word.

Next, they brought me to the guard house. One of them shoved me inside and threw me on a chair. He grabbed a whip and began to strike me. He broke off for a moment to take off my shoes and my hairpins, then took up the whip again. His blows were punctuated with questions. "Who sent you? Where are your friends? What does Issam know?" I stayed mute.

The guard broke off and put me in handcuffs. He left me on the chair, my hands bound. A few moments later, a group of men came in. The guard came back and put a revolver to my temple.

"Talk, or I'll kill you."

"I've already said everything."

In spite of all this, I felt totally calm. I know that later, in his report, César would insist on this point. When he came upon me in the living room, I was quite composed. I was even smiling slightly. It might seem incredible, but I had just been fundamentally transformed. I had rid myself, once and for all, of the mask of the superficial and carefree student. I had lived schizophrenically for so long, never letting down my guard or confiding in anyone apart from M.A. and Rabih. For months, I had lied, tricked, and hid. Now that I had shot Antoine Lahad, I could finally say who I was and what I thought.

At last, faced with my enemies, I no longer had to play a role. The guard sighed.

He took the gun from my temple, removed the bullets from the clip, and picked up his whip. Again he beat me, unmercifully. I screamed in pain.

After what seemed like a long time, there was a knock at the door. Two men came in. The guard put a hood over my head. They bound my feet and took me away. To move, I had to hop with my feet together. I heard a voice. "Look, she can still hop!" The voice spoke again, to me this time. "Well done. You've killed him!" I was grabbed by the shoulders and thrown in the trunk of a car that took off with a screech. We arrived in a place that seemed like the SLA camp, then changed vehicles. They lay me across the back seat of another car. I had the feeling, judging from the road's ups and downs, that we were heading towards Khiam, several miles away. The old military camp had a few years earlier been turned into a prison with an evil reputation. The passenger in the front seat insulted me, piling on words dripping with sexual innuendo. "You slept with the Hasbaya people, you'll see how it goes with us." His hands moved roughly over my body, but I still had the opportunity to bite them. After another stop and another change of car, I landed, sitting, in the back seat. I recognized the voice of at least one person we had picked up. It was Abu Samir, one of the heads of security in Marjayoun, an ex-soldier of the Lebanese Army and a friend of Issam's.

A few miles on, I realized that I was, in fact, being taken to Israel. The matter was too important to leave in the hands of the Lebanese. We crossed the border, then pulled into a kind of barracks. The car came to a stop. I got out and was permitted to remove the hood. They led me into an office. I sat down in a chair, my hands and feet still bound.

A man came in. Later, I learned he was called Tommy. He sat in front of me, and the interrogation began. What was my name? Who had sent me to Marjayoun to kill Lahad? What role did Issam play? I answered the questions in a few words. Then he read off a list of Lebanese names and asked me if I had relations with the Khoury family. I knew no one of that name. Brutally, he threw me on another chair, and tried again. He was particularly insistent about that family name. I repeated my denial. Another man took over and dragged me into another room, slapping me on the way. He threw me to the floor, then turned and left. During the struggle, I had lost a tooth. On the floor on all fours, I stumbled on it, which in spite of everything made me smile. The man came back and the cruelty began again. The Israeli threatened me with all kinds of torture, rape, and above all, with transfer to Khiam. He played with the buttons on my shirt for a moment to give force to his words. But the interrogation ended there.

I was blindfolded again and we left the place. As I had imagined, the Israelis were sending me back to the occupied zone. They didn't want to deal with such a cumbersome prisoner.

After a few minutes' drive, we reached my final destination. I had entered the interior of Khiam, where we had been a short time before. It was just after midnight. I felt like I was in a tent, but later I understood that I was inside, in a barracks. A Lebanese man arrived: Samir, the son of Abu Samir. In the camp, where none of the guards used their real name, his pseudonym was Samer. He was head of interrogations in that special prison. From then on, he would be in charge of my case.

They turned me over to a female guard who undressed and searched me. She led me into one of the rooms used for interrogations.

Still bound and blindfolded, I found myself facing a man. The questions began again.

"What was Issam's true role?"

I protested that my cousin had no knowledge of the operation, but my interlocutor was not at all convinced. He fastened electrodes to my hands and started up a generator. I discovered torture by electricity. The pain made me cry out, louder and louder each time. My torturer slipped a gag into my mouth to shut me up. At other times, I had been accidentally shocked by a live wire or a badly grounded plug, but now the electrical charges were incessant and traveled across my whole body. Immune to my pleading, the man carried on his task, repeating his questions.

"Talk, and I'll stop."

I still held out. Suddenly, he threw water on my hands. The pain became intolerable. I cried:

"Take it off and I'll answer."

He stopped and untied my hands. I hurriedly rubbed them on my clothes to dry them.

"Does Issam work for the resistance?"

"Yes."

Before answering, I had hesitated a moment. I had acted alone, and Issam had absolutely nothing to do with our movement. I knew that I would cause him serious trouble by linking him to this affair, he who was always so careful to look after his interests. But I was overwhelmed by fear, still terrorized by that first session of torture. My only thought was to gain a little time, and above all to end the interrogation. My answer seemed to satisfy the man, although he promised me an even more painful session if I had lied to him.

Six hours had passed since the news of the operation, and the SLA and the security forces had set up a huge dragnet in the occupied zone. Of course, because I was staying with him, Issam was one of the first to be arrested. His wife later tried to slip him a note in Russian, and she was arrested and held for four days. My "confession" didn't hasten their release, to say the least.

My room in Marjayoun was searched from top to bottom. But the first revolver, still hidden in the television set, was not found. A few days later, I had to describe where it was so that the security services could finally get their hands on it.

Soldiers were also sent to Deir Mimas. They arrested my mother as well as my uncle, who had come down for the olive harvest and was staying at our house. My mother was brought for safe keeping to Khiam, where she was held for over a month.

All in all, sixty people close to me were arrested, interrogated, and even tortured. My friend Hanan Khoury was arrested first. When the Israelis had asked me if I knew the Khourys, I had answered in good faith. I had never called my friend anything other than Hanan, to the point of forgetting her last name. The honors for longest detention would go to another friend of mine, Shafika, held for six months, and to Safa, secretary for a pro-Israeli official, arrested and held for forty days. Naturally, none of the people thrown in jail had been aware of my plans.

The first interrogation was over. It must have been around five in the morning. I was led into a cell of around 150 square feet, and the door was locked behind me. The room was not empty. I could make out two mattresses placed on the floor. A young woman was lying on one of them. Woken up by my arrival, she came towards me and asked me my name and the reason for my arrest. I told her that I had killed Antoine Lahad. With a cry of joy she congratulated me, welcoming the news. "They came tonight, at two in the morning, and told me that soon I'd be getting some company," she explained. She was very sweet to me, but I kept myself from being too familiar with my companion in misfortune. Rabih, before leaving, had warned me against friendships made in prison. He knew that the camps were riddled with spies. In the occupied zone, people could be arrested on the flimsiest pretext. Once under lock and key, it was tempting to collaborate with the jailers, especially if one had done nothing wrong. The inmates hoped that a few secrets told to the right person would help shorten their time.

For over two months, the interrogation sessions went on, usually three a day, although they could also be called in the middle of the night. On my arrival, Awad, from Deir Mimas, was the first to interrogate me. Then it was the turn of Wael, from the village of Ayshiya. Next my main interrogator became Samir, with the help of Abu Fares and "Rambo," who changed his pseudonym when he found out that a dog had the same name. A hundred times, a thousand times, I was forced to tell how I had joined the resistance, why Antoine Lahad had been chosen, and how I had organized the operation. These exhausting sessions were interspersed with torture by electricity. The electrodes were nearly always placed on my hands.

Later they would also douse me with buckets of freezing water and leave me there for long hours, bound and shivering, in the middle of winter, which is sharply cold in the mountains of the South.

Little by little, I noted that the parallel interrogations of the people close to me must have been making progress, because the questions I was asked became more specific. I was asked about my anxiety on hearing that my first admirer, Ghassan, a Communist, had been captured by the Israelis during an operation. I had gone to Beirut that day with Issam, who had witnessed my reaction. I realized that Issam must have just described the scene. I could hardly blame him. I could imagine his distress, caught up despite himself in the tumult, along with his wife, Jeannette, herself a prisoner in Marjayoun.

At first I struggled to tell my interrogators as little as possible, or to lead them down false trails. They had fairly detailed knowledge about all my movements in the occupied zone during the previous few weeks, but despite this I lied to them in the beginning about the guns. I told them that they had been given to me in the South. After being tortured several times, I admitted that I had brought them with me from Beirut. This confession brought down terrible curses on me. The same scene was repeated some time later, on another subject. I had told my interrogators in the beginning that my only contact was with a person named Rabih, and I stuck to this story for several weeks. Then, exasperated by Samir's arrogance, who told me every chance he got that he knew everything about me, how I spent my time and every step I had taken in Beirut, I revealed the truth and told them about my original contact with M.A. I was soon classified among the hard cases.

During the first few days of my arrest, I tried to find out what had happened to Antoine Lahad. In Khiam, I was cut off from the outside world, but the closeness of Marjayoun made my task easier. I tried to guess at the comings and goings of vehicles around Khiam, and above all I strained to hear if the bells were ringing there as a sign of mourning—without success. I didn't manage to glean anything concrete. As far as I was concerned, the operation had succeeded. I had hit the militia chief, and Rabih had been unequivocal about the deadliness of the poison. However, I quickly gave myself a harsh critique: after the fact, the idea of limiting myself to two bullets seemed totally ludicrous. I should have seen the business through to the end by relying on the judgment of specialists. It was not my place to impose my own ideas.

Then, during my interrogations, I was constantly corrected when I told my torturers that I had killed Antoine Lahad. "You only tried to kill him," they would reply. At first, I didn't pay much attention, thinking that it was another tactic to throw me off balance. But their persistence began to trouble me. One day, my interrogator took off the blindfold that I wore at all times, showing me diagonally a clipping from the Lebanese newspaper Al Safir. I distinctly made out part of one phrase: "after the attempt to assassinate him, Antoine Lahad..." The guard gloated at me. "You see? You didn't kill him!" The militia leader had been quickly evacuated to Israel, where the doctors had worked miracles. Seriously wounded, he survived, although his left arm remained partially paralyzed.

Later, when I told my interrogator that I could have used a higher-caliber gun, he exclaimed, "With a 5.5, you definitely would have killed him!" So I had not killed the head of the SLA. Still, I was not disappointed. We had still reached our goal of showing the vulnerability of the system that the Israelis had put in place, while letting them know that neither they nor their allies could rest easy anywhere in the occupied zone.

Now I had to devote myself to the essentials. Survival.

10 KHIAM

Khiam, or hell with no name, with no existence.

The Khiam prison, set up in an old military installation, was created in 1985 to replace the Ansar 1 and Ansar 2 camps, which the Israelis had established in 1982 and then abandoned three years later during their partial retreat from Lebanon. Khiam sat on a promontory that was strategically important for the occupied zone. It was far from any fighting, quite close to Israel, and difficult to access. Officially, the SLA was responsible for the prison, although the Israelis had managed it directly when it was created and then gradually shifted the interrogation work to Lebanese mercenaries. Shin Bet, the Israeli internal security agency, kept files on all the detainees, and now and then its agents would come to inspect the premises. The squat buildings of Khiam looked down upon the village of the same name. They consisted of interrogation rooms and two sets of usually overcrowded collective cells, one set for men and one set for women. A few other buildings housed the guards, and that was all. The prison was encircled by watchtowers and surrounded by a minefield. It would have been extraordinarily difficult, if not impossible, to escape.

When I landed there, its reputation was already well established. Of course, both the SLA and Israel denied its existence. But the detainees who were periodically released by the pro-Israeli militias, though told never to speak of it, had already described in some detail the kind of life—if you could call it that—that went on inside. From what scraps of information various human rights groups had gathered, Khiam already held a high place on their list of infamy. Not that it helped.

The occupation, condemned by the United Nations, made South Lebanon a zone with no juridical status, ruling out the possibility of missions by NGOs or international institutions. Even the International Committee of the Red Cross was not authorized to see the prisoners.

The hell of Khiam lay behind closed doors.

The prison fed on two kinds of prey. First there were the resistance fighters, myself among them, captured in battle or exposed by the security forces. We all suffered the same fate. Interrogation and torture to start, then seclusion without trial or sentence, the length of detention set by the whims of the jailers. Israel did not want to appear responsible for these cumbersome detainees. Probably, a part of the Israeli public would not accept such human rights violations committed under the auspices of their country. The proof: when Lebanese were detained on Israeli soil, kept as hostages in exchange for information about soldiers missing in action, or even more macabre, in exchange for the bodies of those killed and abandoned to the enemy, Israeli and Palestinian human-rights groups and lawyers would struggle tirelessly for the prisoners. In comparison, Khiam was perfect for Israel. No laws, no judges, no lawyers. Prisoners in Khiam were negated, buried, conveniently wiped from the world of the living.

But the security forces were not satisfied with locking up the ones who fought them. The prison was often bursting with people who had no relation to the guerrillas. Women, children, and the elderly, from all backgrounds, were also transferred to Khiam for the purposes of intimidation, pressure, and torture. For the SLA, it was a means to get information about people judged to be suspicious, and a way to blackmail or threaten the prisoners into collaborating with the security services in the occupied zone. For these prisoners, too, detention became a kind of lottery. No one knew, on going into Khiam, if he would be released the next week or many years later.

And no one could be sure of coming out alive, particularly the women—the daily routine wore down even the most healthy. In part, this was because of the climate. The prison, located to the south of Beirut but at a high altitude, was stifling hot in summer and freezing cold in winter. Snow would fall at that height, and the buildings, like all those in hot countries, were designed without the slightest protection against the cold. The cells, which naturally had no running water, were spartan. The detainees slept under sheets on old foam mattresses. Blankets were rare. Because of poor construction, the floors of the jail were never clean. Moisture rose from the ground and seeped through the mattresses at night, chilling you to the bone. Apart from these pallets and some iron water-tanks, the detainees shared a plastic bucket, often without a lid, as a latrine. It was emptied twice a day, in the heat of summer as in winter. The buckets were usually constructed out of kitchen-oil jugs. The women, of course, were deprived even of the bare minimum. They had to tear off strips of clothing to make the necessary menstrual pads, then endlessly wash them out, again and again.

In Khiam, the rhythm never changed.

The women detainees were woken at dawn and given a frugal breakfast. They then had to clean their cell, come out by turns and empty the bucket, quickly wash themselves in the cramped room designated for that purpose, and fill up their water-cans. Time outside the cell was limited to five minutes, measured by stopwatch in a quasi-military fashion. Tardiness was severely punished. At noon, a scanty lunch was brought into the cells. In mid-afternoon, a few pieces of food were also served. These three moments were the only times of day when the prison became somewhat animated. At all other times, silence was the rule, and any raised voices were subject to punishment. Coughing, or clearing one's throat, was also prohibited. The detainees could talk in low voices with other women inside the same cell, but communication between cells was not allowed.

The prisoners, shut up in their cells, were cut off from all contact with the outside world. Visits were forbidden, even for families who lived only a few miles from Khiam. Nothing came to lighten the dull monotony. Whether they had been captured during an operation or torn unsuspecting from their beds, the women were all in the same boat. The only things they owned were the clothes they had been wearing when they arrived at the prison. Washed and patched a thousand times, loaned and traded around, they were quickly reduced to a state of rags. In theory, the stock of pants, shirts, and dresses was only replenished by new arrests. But luckily, the families of detainees from the occupied zone were able to smuggle in clothes by giving a few little gifts to the female guards. It was also the custom for a prisoner, if she was released, to leave her sturdiest things for the ones who stayed.

The mediocre food and uncomfortable cells encouraged sickness in bodies already tired out by interrogations and intensive torture. In the prison, where the detainees (men and women) sometimes numbered over two hundred, there were supposed to be two medical orderlies, of extremely limited competence and means, but usually there was only one. In Khiam, you were better off not getting sick. It was very difficult to get permission from the camp authorities to be transferred to the nearest hospital in Marjayoun. You were also better off not complaining too much or breaking the rules. Reprisals were instant. Beatings and time in solitary subdued the more rebellious.

When the men arrived at Khiam, they received regulation clothes, made of the same blue material as the hoods they wore when they left their cells. For the male prisoners, living conditions were even harsher than for the women, partly because of overcrowding and the constant beatings administered by the guards. This was especially true of the solitary cells. A woman confined to solitary was locked up in a sort of box, two and a half feet wide by six and a half feet long and eight feet high, in which she could still move a little. For the men, solitary was a nightmare; the cell was a cube, measuring less than three feet a side, pierced by a tiny hole. The prisoner, swallowed up, compressed, folded over on himself, was of course unable to stand and could barely move except to eat. He was sometimes taken out so that he could hurriedly wash himself. Yet somehow prisoners survived in that half-light for many months, though they often suffered heavy consequences: skeletal disorders and problems of vision. One of them held out for a year and a half of this inhuman treatment.

On top of all this, the sense of solidarity that should naturally have grown between the prisoners was constantly undermined by suspicion. On her arrest, a prisoner was immediately subject to interrogation. Between sessions, she was thrown in a cell, and there she was seldom alone. Her cellmates were always manipulated by the SLA, lured by the prospect of release on condition that they faithfully report whatever secrets they might gather there. I've mentioned how my superior in the resistance, Rabih, put me on guard against these all too friendly and understanding prisoners. They were always on the lookout, taking advantage of the stress and exhaustion of many hours of brutal treatment to tease out information you desperately tried to hide. Scattered through the cells, these "moles" were also able to discover the different tricks and strategies for getting out of punishment or escaping isolation. You had to constantly watch yourself and those around you, try to catch a detainee and a guard exchanging an unexpected word or signal, and then expose the collusion.

The women were often subject to the most intimate kinds of pressure. An interrogation room could be a place of terrible manipulation. One day I learned the story of a young woman, arrested for no particular reason, who had been seduced by one of her interrogators. He managed to convince her to have sexual relations with him, luring her with the prospect of marriage. Won over by his sincerity, she submitted. Probably she also thought that it would help her gain her freedom. She quickly discovered that she had fallen into a trap. The loss of her virginity made her the object of permanent blackmail, even after she had returned to her family. And for her to admit what had happened was out of the question.

For the people shut up in Khiam, the lack of information from outside made them even more easily manipulated. What was going on in Lebanon or in the rest of the world? No one knew much. The detainees depended on scraps of information overheard in the guards' conversation, or very rarely on copies of newspapers, even single pages, pinched on the way to the interrogation rooms or the toilets. The interrogators would also sometimes let slip a piece of information to their victims if it worked in their favor, but you never knew if it was true or only a bluff.

It was like this that I learned fairly quickly about the fall of the Berlin Wall and the Soviet Union, though I was arrested at the end of 1988. Abu Nabil took great pleasure in telling me, thinking he was getting to the heart of my beliefs. He was wrong. I had become involved with the Lebanese Communist Party for reasons that had nothing to do with Marxist theory. Before the operation against Antoine Lahad, I had already seen the beginnings of this decay, and at that moment I honestly didn't feel one way or another about it.

On the other hand, I was very late in hearing of the outbreak of the Gulf War, which followed Iraq's annexation of Kuwait in 1990, and of the end of the Lebanese civil war, which was sealed by the Taif Accord, negotiated in Saudi Arabia one year earlier. The same was true of the Israeli-Palestinian peace process, which, with the Oslo Accords of 1993, ended the intifada that had been so close to my heart.

Beyond the sessions of torture and general ill-treatment, Khiam also went through a particularly intense crisis. In October 1989, the detainees revolted in protest against their living conditions. Then men began banging on their cell doors and chanting slogans, *Allah Akhbar,* "God is great!" The prisoners had lost all hope, but they came together. The movement spread from cell to cell, bringing reprisals from the interrogators and guards. Abu Nabil burst into the women's section and violently grabbed a prisoner named Kifah. She was dragged roughly from her cell and thrown into the guards' room, ending up in the burning coals of the fireplace—luckily more afraid than hurt. Abu Nabil ordered her to tell the other women to be silent. She refused, and was beaten by the guards.

Once again, the men suffered more, choking on tear gas in their overcrowded cells. The informers still in the cells pleaded with the guards to let the wounded out. The prisoners demanded to speak directly with the Israelis. The Israelis arrived a few minutes later, but the riot was just as brutally suppressed. The leaders, or those considered to be so, were tortured horribly.

Two men died during the uprising.

The prison officials made a few improvements after the riot. We were given old Israeli sleeping bags and sanitary buckets. But the men were still only allowed to empty their buckets once a week, and had to resign themselves to the perpetual stench.

On September 7, 1992, an altogether different event took place in Khiam. We were woken that night by a muffled explosion near the outer wall. What was happening? Along with most of the other women, I imagined that an armed group was trying to break into the prison. The alarm was sounded. At first, the guards thought that a stray dog had wandered into the minefield that surrounded the building. Then they made out a wounded man, stuck in the middle of no man's land. They sent up flares, illuminating him. I heard the medical orderly tell a guard to get his gun. The guard said he didn't want to die for the Israelis in that place. Little by little, silence returned to Khiam. The SLA soldiers were barricaded in their shelters, waiting for the Israelis. They came much later, heavily equipped. I recognized the voice of one of them, who questioned the man. The Israelis decided to try and retrieve him, after establishing his identity.

It turned out he was a detainee whose right hand and eye had been blown off by a mine. The man had succeeded in escaping the guards' surveillance, along with three others who had been luckier crossing the minefield. The Israelis deployed some impressive machinery to reach the prisoner. They used huge metal sheets to detect the antipersonnel mines that studded the field. After two hours' work, they managed to cross the twenty feet that separated them. A soldier moved over to the wounded man. He was getting ready to lift him when the voice of Abu Nabil rang out from the prison roof: "Careful! He might be armed!" The soldier, startled, dropped the inmate heavily to the ground. But nothing happened. The man was evacuated to the hospital in Marjayoun.

During this time, other Israelis and SLA militiamen went off in pursuit of the three escapees. Despite all their considerable means, they were unable to pick up the trail in time. One of the three, also wounded during their flight, convinced his friends to abandon him, as he was slowing them down. He was quickly discovered by the Israelis. The two other prisoners, still on the loose, managed to get out of the occupied zone. They were the only ones to escape during my whole time of detention.

The authorities reacted by reinforcing the doors and windows, equipping them with extra bars, and reducing to a bare minimum the detainees' ability to do minor maintenance work on the prison—the men had taken advantage of this to plan their escape. Finally, each night the guards made a thorough search of all the cells.

In my head, I can still hear the sound of the guardsbanging on the windows, testing their solidity.

11 PRISONER

At the age of twenty-one I was brought to Khiam, for how long I did not know.

The first days were exhausting. I was interrogated endlessly about my past and about the operation. I also had to endure the questions of my cellmates—they hoped that by cooperating and giving a few secrets to the female guards, they could win their favor. Ever since that moment, just after the operation, when a revolver had been pressed against my temple, the possibility of being executed on the spot seemed to have diminished, especially now that Antoine Lahad had survived his wounds.

Once, a few weeks after my arrest, I went again before Samir. This time my eyes were not blindfolded. My interrogator asked me very general questions, "journalistic questions," as he called them. He asked me what would be the last thing I would do if I was going to be executed. I told him that I would sing a song by Marcel Khalifé, a song that celebrated the resistance.

Before this, I had known only one real moment of anxiety, also during an interrogation. The session was in progress, when suddenly a wailing siren cut it short. I was ordered to stand, my hands still bound and my eyes covered. I heard people rushing all around me. I was given over to the female guards, who shouted at me to run. On the way, I kept asking, "What is happening? What is happening?" No one knew anything. Finally, I was led back to my cell.

A false alarm.

Through all those weeks, faced with Samir or more rarely one of his associates, I kept lying and shifting stories about anything that concerned only me. I fought the interrogators, rarely holding my ground, often confused by their cross-examination. Right from the first day, I admitted I had lied; less than an hour after casting blame on my cousin Issam, I demanded to see someone so that I could clear him. Later, I lied again about the guns. I claimed that I did not know the revolver was loaded with poisoned bullets, which seemed impossible to my torturers. Every new lie they discovered unleashed a torrent of threats. I was invariably told that if I was found to have misled them, I would suffer terrible consequences. "I'll always be able to find you, even in Beirut, even in twenty years," one of them snarled.

But when I was asked about the information given by those interrogated parallel to me, I denied nothing. Sometimes I would confirm some story or other that intrigued my interrogators. I admitted that, shortly before the operation, I had made an unauthorized visit to the Israeli side of the border accompanying my friend Safa. She worked for the administrative service in charge of distributing passes to Lebanese cross-border workers. We made the incursion with no particular goal in mind, but it shed light on the flaws in the system.

During that period of interrogation, it was like I was sinking into an endless tunnel. The sessions were all the same; I could barely tell them apart. The questioning, the torture by electricity, it all seemed part of the same routine.

Once I was summoned in the middle of the night. Abu Faras ordered me to undress. It was very cold. I slowly began to undo my clothes. Then he gave me the order to stop. Later on, Samir asked me to give him the names of clandestine Party members, but I stuck to making a chart of the official leadership. Later still, my interrogator told me to remove my blindfold. I saw a revolver on the table between us. "Take it!" he ordered me. Obviously, I did not accept the invitation.

Since I had passed through the prison gates, I had discovered violence and pain. When they struck me, or when they turned on the generator that was linked to my body with electrodes, my mind went blank. I thought of nothing, and screamed out my suffering. I dreaded the pauses, when the arm that pulled the lever halted in its course, when their questions threw you into a panic, when you waited in fear for the pain to return.

But even worse was the pain of hearing, from the depths of your cell, the cries of the others, twisting inside your head, leaving you without respite, because you knew what they were suffering there, subject to the same inhumanity, tortured by the same men, humiliated and disfigured by the same savagery.

The sessions became more frequent, but my file did not make much progress.

Once I was interrogated jointly by Samir and Wael. Wael was the chief interrogator for the men, who endured much more cruelty than the women did. He had a terrible reputation. Wael complained bitterly about Samir's ineffectiveness. "Samir doesn't know how to torture you," he said. "With me, it would be different." But the interrogators complied with the strict rules of Abu Nabil, the head of Khiam. I endured only torture by electricity.

In fact, Samir hit me only once. It was after an interrogation done in the presence of my mother, who was also being held prisoner in Khiam.

That day, I was sitting, handcuffed and blindfolded. My mother was brought into the interrogation room. She urged me to give them what they wanted, to tell them how I had planned the operation. "Save yourself, and save us!" she pleaded with me. At that moment, I refused to feel guilty for dragging my family into this mess, even though I feared the consequences for them. By a strange reflex, which in extreme circumstances makes us give weight to things that appear to be of only secondary importance, I feared above all that the parents of my sister's suitor would now oppose their marriage—I knew they didn't care much for the ideals of the Lebanese resistance.

My mother, when she was brought in to see me, was also under tremendous pressure. She saw me, a prisoner, and at the same time the security services were trying to convince her that, since our arrest, her husband was making more and more public appearances for his precious Communist Party—which was a lie. I sat like a stone, unmoving, insensible to her pleas.

After a few minutes, Samir sent her away. Exasperated by my silence, he struck me in the face. I still said nothing.

Later, my mother overheard the interrogators talking. "She's a tough one, all right. She didn't move an inch."

After a few months, my period of interrogation ended. Samir said that my file would remain open, and that any new information would make me subject to questioning. "There's no reason to celebrate," he added. "Now you'll learn what it's like to be dead."

Despite myself, I had grown used to a certain rhythm of life in the prison, and I lost it with the end of the interrogations. I also lost any contact, however hateful and pain-ridden, with non-prisoners. A new kind of struggle for survival was beginning, full of uncertainty and doubt.

I decided to set myself a course.

I had not died with a gun in my hand, and I was not going to be executed, so I had to get ready for a long period of detention. To guide me, I had the year 2000 fixed in my mind. It was a political choice. I thought that by then the Israelis would finally have left Lebanon. Why in twelve years? Because they had moved in twelve years ago. Perhaps because the Lebanese resistance had not weakened since its creation in 1982—far from it—and that sooner or later it was bound to win this war of attrition, fought on its own ground. It was 1988, and so I told myself that I was in for ten years, a round number, twelve at the most. This was what I said, spontaneously, to an Israeli who came in 1990 to question me, when he asked if I thought I would be freed in four years: "Not four, ten!"

I was preparing myself for this far-off appointment when a new test began. The cell in which I had been placed with other girls was just next to the female guards' room. They were constantly bursting into our cell, searching us, shouting at us to be quiet. Now, the only time I left was to go meet the head of Khiam, Abu Nabil. He was a tall man, forty-eight years old, white-haired and mustached. A penetrating look came from his emaciated features. He made me think of a wolf, always on the lookout. He was very impulsive, and to break the will of those with whom he had been entrusted, he was capable of terrible outbursts of violence. Originally, Abu Nabil was from a small village near Marjayoun. He had come to Khiam after serving in the military, at the camp's very beginning, and he soon brought it under his authority.

When I met him, he ordered me to be quieter in my cell, and to convince my cellmates to do the same. My visits to his office caused me trouble with the other detainees, who probably wondered whether I was becoming an informer. When I went before Abu Nabil, I stayed silent. His reprimands were only a pretext; I was not particularly noisy.

Then one day I was dragged brutally from my cell for no apparent reason. I was thrown to the ground and lashed with a studded whip on my legs and on the soles of my feet. I tried to count the blows. After the twelfth, I lost track. Abu Nabil and Wael were standing over me. Wael cried, "Now we won't hear you talk. We won't even hear you breathe." Exasperated by my attitude in the interrogation room, he had decided to break me, to do whatever it would take to make me cooperate.

When I returned, my cell was empty. All my cellmates had been transferred. I found myself alone.

My legs began to hurt. At first, during the punishment, I had not noticed, but it didn't take me long to understand. Some of my wounds were raw, and my limbs were swelling visibly. All night, I forced myself to do exercises, walking up and down, so that the next day I could carry out the prison rituals: cleaning the cell, washing, getting food and water.

In the morning, the pain was unbearable. The female guards took pity on me and offered me the help of another detainee. I refused. I managed, with some difficulty, to carry out my daily tasks. I was alone for three days. I wondered what was happening. One morning, a girl was transferred to my cell. Her name was Maqbulay. She had been arrested almost at random and was in the throes of a serious depression, almost to the point of madness. In shock, closed in on herself, the girl repeated the same words, monotonously, again and again. I tried to question her, to learn more, but it was difficult. She was terrified, with a fear that had become irrational, that her whole family had been arrested and tortured. Her hands were blue from twisting. I tried to take care of her. Fortunately, my own health improved. After the eighth day, I hardly suffered any more.

Soon other girls came to join us.

Quickly, they began to complain about Maqbulay, whose behavior was hard on the nerves. I struggled to come up with distractions, silent group games that would deflect attention from her.

But my trials started again. Abu Nabil definitely had me in his sights—he wanted to make me give in. Another incident only added to my already heavy file. A new prisoner arrived, and I tried to pass her a note warning her against the informers who lurked in the cells. I slipped the paper into the pocket of her pants, which I had seen drying in the room that served as both bathroom and laundry. A little later, the surprised young woman discovered the note, unfortunately in front of her three cellmates. Abu Nabil was of course told about this event without delay. He called for me and assured me that he knew who had written the message.

I was not convinced that he had any proof. Still, I decided to take responsibility for the note. I stood up to the head of Khiam, telling him I would always do as I pleased.

My feelings of persecution and injustice pushed me to revolt, and the answer of my torturer was not long in coming. He announced that from then on I would be bound and placed in solitary. "As long as you refuse to work for us, you will stay there alone," he promised me.

So I was now sentenced to total isolation, solitary confinement. I was put in handcuffs, my hands behind my back, and brought to cell 7, the "little cell," a minuscule box with no mattress or blanket. I was also put on a special diet: one paltry meal served once a day, to be eaten in ten minutes once the cuffs had been removed, along with a single cup of water. In theory, I was allowed to go and wash myself once a week, although they often forgot to take me out of my cave.

I rose to the challenge. I tried exercising to keep my spirits up, but I didn't have enough to eat. Despite having only one meal a day, I decided not to throw myself on my food, but to eat slowly in order to avoid stomach problems. Still, the ten minutes granted to me went by very quickly, and I became visibly thinner. My pants, without a belt, sagged around my hips. By contorting myself, I rapidly learned how to bring my hand-cuffed wrists under my feet and back in front of me. This helped me sleep less badly, although each morning I had to be careful to wake up in time to assume the "regulation" position, in case I had a visitor.

After two weeks, a guard who entered my cell to bring me my soup had some trouble taking off my handcuffs. I told her I had another solution: I could bring my hands in front of me. She was skeptical, and asked me to show her. In a few movements I had done it. I knew that she would probably go tell Abu Nabil, but I wanted to show him that I would not waver. That same night, Wael came to see me. Abu Nabil had decided to cuff me in a particularly uncomfortable position: my right wrist to my right ankle. "Are you happy? That's better, now," my torturer jeered at me and turned on his heel. In answer, I forced a smile.

This was a cruel new punishment.

I had trouble getting even the most minimal exercise. I could no longer stand up. Luckily, I was saved by the decrepit equipment itself. The cuffs kept getting stuck when the guards tried to remove them before bringing me to the room which served for washing up. Tired of struggling, they eventually took them off for good. I could resume a normal position, but I remained alone in my cell. I still tried to exercise, hoping to stay strong in spite of the circumstances. Every day, I walked the equivalent of two or three miles. Because of limitations of space, it was a complicated maneuver that required some concentration. From the rear of the cell, my back touching the wall, it was just two steps to the door. I had to pivot around, take two more steps, then pivot again, repeating this movement thousands of times, while trying to keep enough presence of mind not to bump into a wall.

In December 1989, I got my second piece of "good news," after the removal of the handcuffs. I was presented with a mattress and a blanket. At once, my cell took on the air of a five-star hotel. It was pure bliss for my weary thighs, which had turned blue from so many uncomfortable nights.

My first period in solitary ended after ten months. It would not be the last. Later, I would alternate between solitary cell 7 and solitary cell 24, which was slightly less cramped.

During those ten months, Abu Nabil twice interrupted my isolation. The first time he sent for me, it was to offer me a deal—he said I could take it or leave it. The Israelis were looking for Ron Arad, the pilot who had disappeared over Lebanon. They suspected that Hezbollah had captured him, and hoped that I could help move things along by signing a request for his release. He told me: "When the wind blows, the wheat bends to let it pass, then rises again." His efforts to get me to agree were useless. "You'd be helping everyone in the prison!" he exclaimed. But I refused to be blackmailed, and rejected the term "prison." "I am in a camp," I said. "A prison is a place where people are sent after being tried. With us, this is not the case."

Abu Nabil then suggested that I write letters, which he himself would ensure were delivered. My first thought was for my family. I wrote and asked them to try and understand my actions against Antoine Lahad, advising them to go on with their lives as if nothing had happened, and above all not to make any special pleas with our enemies for my release. Next, I wrote to the President of the USSR, Mikhail Gorbachev, and to the Secretary General of the United Nations, whose name I didn't know. I described at length our deplorable living conditions, especially the lack of proper sanitation. I was sure that my letters went no farther than the Israeli office in charge of Khiam, but I wanted to make them face up to their responsibilities. My third letter was addressed to the Secretary General of the Lebanese Communist Party, and to all parties of Lebanese patriots. In a short text, I urged them all to focus their efforts on fighting the Israeli occupation. I would have been very surprised if the letter reached Beirut.

As a matter of fact, Abu Nabil was not at all happy with what I had written. He ordered me to ask the Communist Party to intercede on behalf of Ron Arad. I wouldn't yield. Instead, I used the pen he gave me to draw flowers and hearts all over my jeans. He immediately responded by confiscating my pants, replacing them with a *gelabiya*, the long robe traditionally worn in the Middle East.

The second time Abu Nabil called for me was to tell me that an interview was going to be arranged with a journalist. He strongly recommended that I tell him everything was all right in Khiam, that I was well treated, and even allowed to take walks outside. Next I met with an Israeli, who questioned me at length. He asked me what I would do when I was released from prison. I repeated the distinction I made, on principle, between a prison and a detention camp, which made Abu Nabil lose his temper. "She keeps telling us this!" he cried. The Israeli didn't linger over this detail, and brought up the name of Ron Arad. I said that he was none of my business.

Two days later I was made to take a shower, and once again a hood was placed over my head. It was time for the interview. Handcuffed and hooded, I left my cell. After a short walk inside the prison, I was told I could take off the hood. I found myself in a large courtyard surrounded by barbed wire. In front of me, four men sat behind a table: Abu Nabil, César, a photographer, and a man I didn't know, evidently the journalist. He asked me if I could speak in French. I replied that I would prefer Arabic, but despite this he insisted that I continue in French. His first questions were about the operation. How had I made my decision? Did I regret it? Would I be ready to do it again? Abu Nabil told us to hurry; our time was limited. Next the journalist wanted to know what I thought about the practice of hostage-taking. I explained that I had always been against it.

I chose my words carefully. The journalist could only have come to Khiam with the blessing of the Israelis, and I strongly doubted that it was a one-sided gesture on their part. More likely, it was another try to help Ron Arad's case. After the interview, which lasted barely twenty minutes, the journalist took a few pictures of me. He told me, before leaving, that his name was Roger Auque, and that he himself had been held hostage by Hezbollah in Lebanon. Finally, he asked me if I had any message to send to my family. I told him to say that I was well, and that I hoped they were getting on with their lives as they had always done.

Much later, I was able to read his article. I didn't agree with what he wrote, but thanks to it my parents learned that I was still alive.

After this unusual visit, I returned to the silence of Khiam.

12 KIFAH

There were also other prisoners in the camp, condemned to the same solitude.

One morning, I left the "little cell" to go to the shower room, flanked by two guards. Once inside, I undressed and was getting ready to bathe, when my fingers brushed against something tucked inside the shower sponge. Without alerting the warders, I managed to slip a small rectangular object—evidently a piece of cardboard—into one of my shoes. I washed myself like nothing had happened, my heart beating wildly. After finishing, I hoped to get back to my cell and examine my treasure in secret, but I was sent for by Abu Nabil. He was not alone—Tommy, the Israeli whom I had met before, was with him. Abu Nabil noticed that I seemed troubled.

"What's the matter with you? What's going on? You look upset."

"I'm always upset when I meet an Israeli!"

Our short exchange ended, and I was finally returned to my cell. I snatched the precious trophy from my shoe. But what a disappointment—the cardboard was totally blank! Dumbstruck, I turned it over and over in my hands. It wasn't possible—I couldn't have been given this cardboard for no reason. After a moment, by angling it towards the light, I managed to make out a few words of encouragement carved into the surface, probably using a piece of wire. It was a message of support from my friend Kifah.

Kifah was not a detainee like any other. Like me, she had fought for the resistance. She was captured in battle, in the middle of an operation against the Israelis. Most importantly,

Kifah was Palestinian, not Lebanese. She had grown up in Beirut, in the Sabra and Shatila camps. She was there in 1982, when the camps came under attack by the militias of the "Lebanese Forces" after the Israeli army entered Beirut. She was eleven years old at the time. She survived the massacre, although three of her brothers were killed. At the age of seventeen, she joined the Palestinian fighters. On October 24, 1988, her group left to carry out an operation, an attempt to capture Israeli soldiers for an eventual exchange of prisoners. Things went badly, and the group fell back to the occupied zone, taking refuge with a Lebanese family. Unfortunately, the father of the family worked for the security services. By the time some members of the group came upon a document proving this link, it was too late—the house was surrounded. After a brief exchange of fire, Kifah and her friends surrendered. They were all handled roughly and transferred to Israel for interrogation, ending up in Khiam.

When I arrived, I had already heard of Kifah, and I knew what she had tried to do. Because of her attempted action and all the excitement it generated in the occupied zone, I even had to push my own project back by a couple of weeks. Kifah had been tortured very harshly in Khiam, but she had managed to hold out. Inside the camp, I spotted her right away. She was eighteen years old, smart and determined, a dark-haired slip of a girl with sad eyes and a brilliant smile. Lively and attractive, she had been the object of much attention before her arrest. She was religious, wore the veil, and tried hard to be a good Muslim.

After we were put in the same cell, we quickly became fast friends. We had much in common: both of us were fearless, young, and committed to the cause. She had no better relations with Abu Nabil than I; we were his two punching bags. Kifah too was allowed to meet with journalists—some Egyptians from Associated Press who even left her a bit of money.

We had agreed to keep in contact even if we were separated, which is what happened when Abu Nabil decided to put me in solitary. We made an appointment, saying that we would try to use the shower room as our letter box.

Before arriving on the day when I found the first note, a cough from Kifah had put me on the lookout. There was mail waiting for me.

"How are you? I'm worried about you. If only I could take your place!" Kifah's words made my heart well up. I answered straight away: "Don't worry about me because I'm in the 'little cell.' Life is good, in spite of everything." I left my letter tucked inside the shower sponge, our mailbox, and I warned Kifah by myself letting out a cough.

In the prison, we had grown used to hanging on the slightest noise, to the point where we had all become specialists of sound. We could identify the step of each guard, the creak of each door. With our ears always on the alert, we could reconstruct all the movement that went on inside the prison, helped by the shadows that passed through the thin crack of light under each cell door. We could tell who was on their way to be interrogated, who was going with them, who came back, and who was transferred. Clearing your throat was a perfect signal, a way to draw attention to some kind of subterfuge that you had planned ahead of time.

From then on, Kifah and I wrote to each other twice a week, on average, whenever I was put into solitary. It all depended on how much "paper" and "pencil" we were able to get a hold of. The best technique was to use the packaging for the foil-wrapped cheese, made in France, which we received once a week. If you rolled the foil up, it made a pretty decent pencil, as long as you were patient and nimble-fingered enough. Kifah and I quickly found another hiding-place: the rubbish bin in the shower room. We had to work quickly, as time was short and the jailers didn't easily let their guard down. But in this way, I was able to find all the supplies necessary to keep up our exchange.

Letters weren't the only way we kept in touch. I soon discovered the possibilities offered by the "little cell." The cell was indeed cramped, but it was also quite high-ceilinged, and at the top was a rectangular window, that as far as I could tell measured around 1 1/2 by 2 feet, blocked by heavy bars. The walls were so close together—just three feet apart—that I was able to hoist myself all the way up to the top. There, I could open the windowpanes and hang on to the bars. When I was hanging at my window, I could see into the courtyard below, which was adjacent to the interrogation rooms and the girls' shower-room. Under the right circumstances, I could even catch a glimpse of Kifah, and we would grin at each other.

I loved my window.

Sometimes I would climb up at night and shake out my blanket, trying to air it out a bit. My window was the perfect way to break the feeling of claustrophobia instilled by such an inhuman place. Every time I looked out, I felt like I was playing tricks on Abu Nabil, ruining his strategy of trying to make me cooperate with him. It was an unexpected and endless source of energy.

Or so it seemed.

The beautiful adventure of my window ended abruptly. One of my interrogators, who happened to glance at the rooftops of Khiam, discovered me perched up there. Immediately, the camp authorities sprang into action. I was dragged from my cell and hauled over the coals by Abu Nabil. I wondered what would become of me, thinking I would probably be moved somewhere else. When they brought me back to my old familiar cell, I was surprised to find it bathed in blue light. The window had been blocked up, covered with a coat of paint. My window was no more—at least for a little while, since the paint soon began to flake off.

Luckily, I still had Kifah.

When we were put together in the same cell, between two of my stints in isolation, we talked endlessly about ourselves, our dreams and desires. We also compared stories. Kifah told me about how, in Israel, she had received some unexpected help from one of her "enemies." She had been interrogated without pause and severely tested. In a cell during a break, she asked her guard—a woman—if she could have something to drink. The guard left without a word. When she came back, she had a quarter of an orange with her, and waited for my friend to drink the juice so that she could then dispose of the skin. I then told

Kifah how I too had been deprived of water during my first three days in solitary. I resigned myself to asking my guard, who was Lebanese, for some water—something I had tried to resist with all my strength. But when I did ask her, she refused.

Unlike many of the prisoners in Khiam, who had been detained in order to blackmail them or turn them into collaborators, Kifah and I knew why we were there. We had made our choice. Still, we worked hard not to keep ourselves separate from the others, and to try to help those who had the hardest time with the camp's injustices.

We went through many trials together, companions in war and suffering. There were the wounds of the soul, like Kifah's despair when she told me about how, under torture, in order to hide the fact that she had been the leader, she had claimed to have joined her group of *fedayin* only for the money. She even repeated this to the Egyptian journalists, who had questioned her in the presence of her torturers.

Even more painful were the wounds of the body, like the eczema that ravaged Kifah's skin. I would plead with her to resist the urge to scratch, she bled so easily. My Kifah—when she came back from torture, she was always in pieces.

My correspondence with Kifah helped keep me out of trouble while I was in solitary. One day, some prisoners started a hunger strike, protesting against the conditions under which two girls were held in isolation. Ordinarily, Kifah and I were against this practice, since it only made sense if you were willing to take it to the limit. We also knew that in Khiam, any effort of this kind would be followed by a series of interrogations and torture to try and find out who started it and the real reasons behind it. Despite everything, I joined the strike, but shortly after it began I got a note from Kifah telling me to stop. She explained that she and her friends were not on a complete strike. They had hoarded some food and ate in secret. Kifah suspected that I wasn't eating a thing.

Thanks to her signal, I stopped in time.

We parted company in the best way possible—after six months of trials but also of friendship. I remember the day, it was August 3, 1994. Her release had become a pressing matter for the Israelis. Kifah's lawyer, an Israeli named Leah Tsemel, had managed through her persistence to get Israel's Supreme Court to hear the case. It was an embarrassing business, and the Israeli authorities wanted it cut short. Kifah also had history on her side. A year after the Oslo Accords, signed in 1993, the Palestinians were trying to get their new partners to release their female prisoners.

At the time, I was in solitary, yet again. I hadn't gotten the "little cell" this time, but another, slightly larger one. I was listening, as always, when I heard the guards' telephone ring. A guard was called for. She left, then returned. I climbed to the window that lit my cell, where I could hear her voice. "There's going to be a release," she announced.

From my observation post, I could see her and another guard stride across the courtyard and stop in front of a cell. They opened the door and called the first girl. "Farida!" She jumped out almost immediately, spying me and signaling to me subtly with her hand. She would be brought to one last interrogation. The guards moved on to another cell, and took out Mouna. Then they stopped in front of a final cell. They called a third name: "Kifah!" Hanging at my window, I heard it like a blow to my chest. My friend moved incredulously to the door. I coughed discreetly one last time, but she was so overwhelmed, she heard nothing. Then, flanked by our guardians, she left.

She was gone.

Two other girls had gone with her. It was the most directly political release of prisoners in my time in Khiam. I was still there, but I knew that as she left, Kifah was taking a small bundle with her.

She had some things of mine in there, and I told myself that they, too, would now be free.

13 TO CREATE

To not waste my time.

This was the goal I set for myself when I arrived in prison: to try to make the most of my circumstances, to learn from them. I didn't want to be bound by the endless waiting that saps the will. I wanted to have control over how I spent my days. After my interrogations had ended, when I finally discovered the "normal" life of the detainees, I quickly realized that it would be hard to put this program into practice.

We were all in a state of extreme want. We had hardly any clothes, no books, and of course no paper or pencil. Khiam was set up in such a way as to leave us, in theory, with no way to distract ourselves, nor any way to escape from the daily regime imposed by the guards. On top of this, most of the girls drugged themselves with sleep, getting as much as they could day and night. At mealtimes, they threw themselves on the food, eating at top speed before falling back into their torpor, though eating was our only source of entertainment. We were cut off from the outside world, and the only activity left to us was to strain our ears trying to follow the movements of the guards and the prisoners from one cell to another, trying to guess who was going where.

When the guards watched soap operas on their little television set, each of us struggled to catch the dialogue. By putting together the spoils of everything we'd heard, we tried to reconstruct the day's episode, though we rarely achieved our goal. Once at least, I had the mixed blessing of a whole evening of Egyptian cinema. I was in solitary, in cell 24, and from my observation post at the window I could make out some scenes on the television of a Cairo-made comedy. I clung to the bars as long as I could, hoping to tell the other girls about it later, in detail and as discretely as possible. But this was practically a punishment.

Luckily, I had some less profane ways to occupy myself. The vast majority of the other detainees were Shiite Muslim, and with them I had the chance to discover a holy text that I previously knew little of: the Koran. They knew the verses by heart, which allowed me to learn them in turn. Because of the environment I grew up in, I wasn't exposed to much religion. So I took advantage of this instruction, free as it was.

In the camp, deprived of everything, we became thieves—thieves of everything and nothing, because even the tiniest piece of stolen paper was a treasure. It was only a short journey from our cell to the shower room or the interrogation rooms, but during those few minutes our eyes roamed wildly. We became experts in stealing the plastic bags that were used to deliver our flat bread. We often converted these bags into emergency toilets, throwing them in the garbage in spite of this being forbidden by the guards, or tossing them through the bars into the no-man's-land surrounding the camp. In addition to plastic bags, we stole scraps of paper, bits of pencil, and little pieces of wire.

Our hands had become scavengers.

We also stole in order to create, to try to make little things without the guards noticing. We had to sacrifice a piece of clothing to get some wool or cotton thread, but with that, we could knit. Aside from the thread, we could count on a supply of olive pits. This was not true for the men—for them, the guards would actually look at their empty plates, checking that the number of pits matched the number of olives they had been given in their rations. The pits could be smoothed and carved, then turned into prayer beads. But all of our materials were simply not enough.

One day, however, we found a nail stuck to the bottom of a shoe, and it let us work wonders. We could make a needle! We worked in shifts through the whole night, rubbing the nail's steel point into a piece of copper electrical wire found in a cell. By daybreak we couldn't feel our hands, but we had done it. There was a hole, an eye, in the copper wire. It had become a needle, and it was going to come very much in handy. For us, it was a huge step forward. We had already tried to make needles out of the teeth of a comb, but everything we made had proved too fragile.

Our sewing had been first of all a product of need. We made our own sanitary napkins (at least until I demanded of Tommy in 1992 that they be provided), and we patched up our clothes. To do this work, we could ask for needle and thread from the guards, but then we had to sew in front of them and give the tools back to them when we were done. We also had to work against the provocations of the interrogators: they would confiscate the headscarves of the Muslim girls, trying to destabilize them and force them to cooperate. One day, as a sign of solidarity and defiance, we manufactured a type of hat for nine of the women, using old sweaters. This headgear looked less like the traditional veil and more like something out of Robin Hood, but it did the trick.

The needle was a huge step forward in our technology, and it freed us to create. For me, creativity was not at all about killing time—it was not just a way to play. To create was finally to reclaim our freedom of expression, to speak our thoughts when everything around us was telling us to be quiet and forget who we were. I was a scientist by training and by vocation, and inside the walls of Khiam, I discovered this irrepressible desire. The objects that we made in secret were messages, and each of us put what she wanted inside. There were, of course, words of love for those dear to us, for our parents and our friends. There were also political words, messages for our country and our cause.

It was our only freedom.

My first object was a rosary of olive pits. It wasn't for prayer. I just liked the shape—I thought it was pretty. I carved the initials of the National Liberation Front into each pit, just out of sheer caprice. My second object was a badge I made from a cigarette filter, which I cut open, fanned into a flower-shape and then knitted with wool. Once again, I drew the initials of the Front on my little badge. I quickly made up a set of cards. I was the only one who knew any games, and I taught them to my fellow inmates. Later there were checkers and chess sets, but sadly, I found no partner to share these passions.

All our efforts were periodically reduced to nothing by the guards, who would search the cells and confiscate anything they found. The cards became "legal" in 1989, but everything else was forbidden. We returned to a cell that had just been searched with our hearts pounding, hoping that at least one precious object had escaped the raid and had not ended up in the garbage with the rest of the spoils.

When you were put in solitary, this ability to throw off the yoke was put to the test. The first few times I was shut away in cell 7 or 24, I had nothing on hand. I had hidden two needles in the collar of a very tight-fitting sweater that only I could wear, but I didn't hurry to ask for it back. I told myself that any urgency would look suspicious, and could give the guards the idea of examining the sweater a bit too closely. It was also extremely difficult to find a hiding-place for my poor treasures. The rooms were empty, especially the "little cell," where at first I didn't even have a mattress. In the beginning, I compensated by doing exercises. But when my wrist and ankle were cuffed together, causing me so much pain, it became impossible to move. I could do a few abdominal exercises, but this was no cure.

I was reduced to immobility, but not yet to inactivity.

In the "little cell," my first reflex was to work on math problems, helped by crumbs of bread, which I stole during the meal and hid in my *gelabiya*. I made up tables of numbers which had equal sums when added vertically, horizontally, and diagonally. Starting with squares of 9 numbers, I worked my way up to squares of 49 numbers, not without some satisfaction. Using a piece of soap, I managed to make a die. Next came a huge project: the creation of a whole board game, the Game of Peace. It combined a kind of snakes-and-ladders game with strategies for conquering territory. The rules were complicated but precise. You had to beat both snakes and soldiers in order to win. It took me a long time to create it, especially since I never stayed long in the same cell. I was in solitary number 24 when I managed to pass the game—finally completed—to my friends. The only weak point was the solidity of the die. When I heard some stifled shouts, it often meant that the key piece in the game had broken after being thrown with too much enthusiasm. Luckily, my fellow prisoners came up with an answer: a clothespin, which they pocketed and then filed down. It turned into a die that could withstand anything.

Our artistic side was also stimulated by what the men created, thanks to the sympathy of one of the guards. She would smuggle objects to us that had been made on the men's side and then confiscated. Their work, which was much more sophisticated than ours, left us speechless. You could see it clearly in the olive-pit prayer beads, which they embellished by covering with cotton or wool. They would also make little hearts out of wool and cardboard. The medical orderly used an original method to slip me one of their models. A heart, which had been confiscated on the men's side, wound up hanging around the neck of the cat that roamed freely through the prison. I actually managed to get the animal to come to me, but the guards caught me in the act and alerted Abu Nabil. He interrogated me about the heart and where it came from. I told him that I had made it entirely by myself.

As much as possible, we tried to give each other presents. I quickly became adept at making pictures, images of all kinds and colors. I sacrificed a pair of pants for my first work. Using wool thread, I sewed in a very stylized representation: two hands clutching the prison bars, with a quill perched on an inkwell in the foreground. I dedicated the picture to a fellow detainee. As a final flourish, I added a short text about our future liberation. I went on to make many pictures, mixing symbols with political slogans that became more and more general. One of them featured the French word *humanité*. I was so sure of the superiority of women when it came to this subject,

I spelled it *humanitée,* adding an extra feminine *e* at the end.

But such feats were only possible when my hands were free, and not when they were trapped in handcuffs. During my time in isolation, I became attracted to the abstraction of poetry. This was not a light-hearted choice—at school, I was a keen mathematician, but as a would-be poet I was always pretty terrible. I wasn't interested in contemplating nature, or gazing at the sky and waiting for inspiration to strike—the idea I had of this literary genre. Still, along with my fellow prisoners, I had learned a poem that one of them had written. When I found myself shackled and in solitary, I tried my luck at this poetic exercise. I soon developed a taste for it, and poetry became a fundamental part of my life in Khiam.

I composed, I fiddled and polished, and when I liked a poem I tried to memorize it. I would repeat it again and again, learning it by heart. As I put myself into my poems, my poems began to live in me. I learned to love them, to make them mine. All together, I composed over fifty poems, forever burnt into my memory.

The first one came to me under dramatic circumstances. A detainee was being tortured; her screams of pain froze me with terror and brought tears to my eyes. I thought again of those interrogators, how they were always bragging about Israel's superiority, its modernity and strength. I denounced that shining star of progress, so capable of crushing human beings beneath its feet, and I celebrated the martyrs and the insurgents who would free us from this yoke.

My second poem was inspired by another torture session that I observed while hanging at my window. An interrogator, worn out by his dirty work, called for a guard to come watch over his victim. Without any reason, the guard began to strike the prisoner, who screamed horribly. Watching this, I composed a poem in memory of my cousin Loula, who had died while on a mission. She was known as "the Pearl of the Bekaa Plain." I described how it was fear that made us cower in the corner of a cell, prostrate, turned in on ourselves, and how

Loula's martyrdom held out the promise of our freedom.

My poems were not only political. I also described the conditions of life in Khiam, the stories of the female guards, and the friendships that bound me to some of the detainees, my dear Kifah among them. Of course, I dedicated a poem to my parents. Lastly, two of my compositions allowed me to describe my vision of love.

I learned my poems by heart, and then strove to carve them into the wall of my cell. This system improved when I could use foil to write on the cardboard packages of cheese. But the best present I was ever given in Khiam was a Bic pen, stolen from the interrogators and given to me one day by my friends, who left it in one of our hiding-places. The pen practically changed my life. Now I could set down all my ideas on the toilet paper they gave us, or of course on pieces of cloth that I recycled as stationery. I was afraid of being searched, so I tried to make as many copies of my poems as possible. My fears were justified, as over and over again the guards would come and confiscate the copies I made.

Armed with my pen, I was not just limited to poetry. On August 3, 1994 (the day that Kifah was released), once again alone in cell 24, I began to write a book. With toilet paper as my parchment, I set down words that had long been brewing in my mind. I tried to organize my thoughts around the idea of my country. Much of what I wrote was about resistance, what it meant to us, and the duties it imposed. When a group of girls went free, on July 21, 1996, another idea came to me: to keep a prison journal. Every day, I tried to record what was going on in Khiam, scrutinizing every unusual event.

Again, it was a question of survival.

14 VISITORS

Some were freed, and when they left, it changed the lives of those who stayed.

When Kifah and the other prisoners were released in August 1994, the atmosphere in the prison shifted imperceptibly. Their release made a deep impression on the girls, giving hope to those who lacked it. The worst, we thought, might still be avoided. At that point, we didn't know that committees of support had been set up (especially in France), that the Israeli lawyers who were working tirelessly to rescue us from oblivion were gaining ground, and especially, that pressure from international organizations on our behalf was becoming more insistent. A year after my best friend was released, the prison gates were opened to visitors, not just officials from the SLA or the Israeli Army.

One Monday evening in September, the guards told Haniya, who was held in the cell next to mine, that she was going to receive a visit from her parents. Haniya was a Hezbollah militant from the occupied zone. She was now in her sixth year of detention, having been locked up in Khiam six months after myself. Secretly, she called to me. She was overwhelmed, torn between joy at finally being able to meet with her parents, and disappointment on hearing of the strict conditions for the visit. "I can only see them from far away, in a room divided by bars," she despaired. "We can't even embrace or touch each other." This gift came out of the blue. It wasn't just limited to the women; the men learned at the same time that they would be allowed to see visitors, too. There were more of them, so they were only allowed ten minutes each to speak, while the women were given half an hour.

Haniya asked herself how she would feel. Her father was quite old, and she wondered how the visit would go with him. The next day, Tuesday, she went to the meeting with a tightness in her throat. Faced with her parents, it was all she could do to hold back her tears; at the same time, she didn't want to encourage their concerns by giving a bad image of herself. She was not alone in this. Everyone around her was paralyzed by emotion. The guards asked them nicely to talk now and keep the sobbing for later. "Hurry up, make the most of it, the time goes by quickly," they repeated endlessly, to those people who faced each other, for the first time in years, in silence.

Words came out haltingly. Haniya had been given some advice before being put in front of her family. She was not supposed to talk about politics, nor about what she had endured in Khiam, or the meeting would be ended immediately. She was supposed to say that everything was fine, to ask about her parents' health and about family news: births, marriages, and deaths.

When my neighbor got back to her cell, I pricked up my ears.

Haniya was already in tears as she crossed the threshold. Between sobs, she described the scene to me, her joy at seeing them all there.

The International Committee of the Red Cross (ICRC) had won a first, hard-fought victory. Through their stubbornness, they had finally gained families the right to visit their detained relatives. The ICRC had also won an improvement in our living conditions. Until then, the prisoners were only allowed to receive a few articles of clothing, and only if their families lived in the occupied zone. Now all Lebanese families had the right to send packages of clothing and food. The family would bring a package to one of the ICRC offices scattered across Lebanon, and the ICRC would compile the packages and bring them over to Khiam. After inspection, they were handed over to the prisoners. The first packages were not of food, but of soap, tissues, and shampoo. For us, it was a revolution. Later on came cookies, sweets, sugar, coffee, dried fruit, and the seeds that everyone snacks on in the Middle East.

The day after Haniya's visit, on Wednesday, there was another dramatic surprise. For the first time, the detainees would be allowed to receive mail. From cell to cell, the news spread like wildfire. The guards gave me a letter, and told me to read it out loud. It was a standard ICRC form that only had room for a short message, barely a dozen lines. I recognized my father's handwriting. I wanted to read it, but the words caught in my throat. The guards gave me a pen, then left me in peace. I only had a quarter of an hour to scribble out an answer. In a neighboring cell, two of the three girls were illiterate, so a single letter was copied out three times, with only the names changed. It was the quickest way to respond in such a short time. The one girl who could write gently rebuked a fellow prisoner, telling her to stop crying and to give her the names of her family.

I quickly wrote out an answer, then reread my father's letter. Of course he was the one who had put pen to paper—it didn't surprise me. I recognized his well-balanced style. In a few words, he told me how he had been able to write, and gave me news of my family, especially of my mother. He told me about the new children who had come into the lives of my brothers and my sister. He assured me that everything was going well at work. Finally, he said he hoped I would soon be free. For him, this first letter was a positive sign. I replied in a playful tone. I wrote that my spirits were high, and that his letter had filled me with joy. I said that I was eating well, and that whenever I wanted for something, like an onion to go with my *foul*—the traditional Middle-Eastern bean soup—I simply had to whistle, and my neighbors would pass me the missing ingredient by way of the guards.

It was a remarkable letter for me—the first time I had ever written to my family.

A day later, it was my turn to be taken from my cell. "Get in the shower," I was told. I had just taken one the day before, so I had the feeling that I too was going to have a visitor. They brought me to the interrogators. Samir asked me if I could guess what was going to happen. I answered that I thought I was going to see some people from the Red Cross. Samir corrected me. "No, you're going to see your mother. You see? We're decent people, not assassins like you. You'll see your mother, but not a word about politics or prison conditions, or we stop everything."

The next day, I chose my clothes with care, putting on the scarf and sweater that Kifah had left me. I knew that when my mother returned, my friend would ask after me, and that my mother would describe the scene to Kifah in detail. I thought that this little signal to Kifah would make her happy.

They put a hood over my head and I left the cell. They led me to a room which was divided down the middle by steel bars. On my side were many people: practically all the interrogators, as well as a man with his face covered whom I quickly recognized as Wael. A door opened in front of me. My mother appeared. On her knees, she moved towards me, up as far as the bars. She had vowed that if she ever saw her daughter alive again, she would approach her like this. She kept her word. She was wearing a skirt, a blouse and a light jacket. I immediately thought that she was not dressed warmly enough, and that she must be cold. I also noticed that her hair had grown white.

"How are you, my daughter?"

"I'm well. And you?"

We plunged into conversation. She asked me if she looked very different, then gave me news of my brothers, my sister, and their children. I reacted straight away, begging her never to bring the children here. Then my mother addressed the onlookers like a courtroom lawyer, launching into an emotional plea. "My daughter is not a terrorist. She is a hard-working student. She loves her studies. She deserves to be released so that she can go back to the university. What's past is past." She passionately declared herself ready to meet, then and there, with the head of the SLA himself—my victim, Antoine Lahad. I broke in: "Mother, this is not the right time."

Our conversation continued. Then a guard interrupted us: "Time's up." My mother put her hand on one of the bars and asked me to do the same. I knew it was forbidden, and I didn't try. The guards were already taking me away when my mother rummaged in her bag, crying: "I brought you a sandwich!" As I was led out of the room, I tried to reassure her that I had everything I needed. I will never forget the sight of her eyes, and her hands clinging to the steel bars.

Back in my cell, I took stock of those incredible days. The women and men who had been detained the longest were the first to receive the privilege of these meetings. But, prudently, I kept myself from building castles in the air, refusing to imagine a swift release.

The arrival of the first letters changed the prisoners. I heard the men talking in loud voices, sharing news of their families, describing their hopes and feelings. But I knew that the letters and the visitors could be used by Abu Nabil as a means of putting pressure on us. I also told myself that, in any case, I would probably have no more visits like this before my release from prison. As far as my release was concerned, it was more unforseeable than ever. I knew that while the International Committee of the Red Cross could visit the detainees, it had no power to free them.

As 1995 began there was renewal in the air, in the form of renovations inside the prison. Three of the women's cells were done up in incredible luxury—that is to say, complete with sinks and summary toilets. Old Israeli-made iron beds, intended for army use, were also distributed—but not to me. Abu Nabil was going to make me ask for one myself. The women guards were always pushing me to do it, but for me, soliciting anything from the head of Khiam was totally out of the question. A month after the first visitors had come, my enemy appeared before my cell. He called a guard, and ordered me to follow her. I was going to get a bed. I figured this meant that something new was going to happen.

The next morning, they opened my cell and told me to present myself at the door. There was a welcoming committee a few feet in front of me. I recognized Abu Nabil, several male and female guards, and the military head of the camp—a total of seven people. They flanked a group of four unknowns, each of whom sported the badge of the International Committee of the Red Cross. As he saw me, the leader of this little group exclaimed in French, "You must certainly be Soha!" We talked quickly for two minutes. The same man, Baltazar, told me news of my mother, who had just broken her leg, then announced that he would soon be back. Amer, the military head of Khiam, confirmed his words.

My door closed again.

The first visit of the ICRC picked up again the next day, continuing until all the prisoners were inspected like this.

The ICRC kept its word, and from then on made regular visits to Khiam. Baltazar had negotiated access to the prison with Antoine Lahad himself, and he managed to push his advantage even further. Shortly after our first meeting, a member of the Swiss organization was given permission to enter the cells and talk with the prisoners. One morning, in spite of the guards' misgivings, Clara made her way into my lair. She was an attractive young woman in her thirties who understood Arabic, expressing herself fluently in that language. She told me how happy they were, after all those years of trying, and how they would do everything they could to improve our lot. She then asked me about the conditions under which I was held. At one point, I saw that my story had moved her to tears. She asked more questions and took a great many notes. Next, I saw a doctor. I drew his attention to the awful state of sanitation in the prison, and told him how the sessions of torture caused serious bleeding in menstruating women.

Another interview was set up, this time in an empty cell. I described in detail my arrest, the interrogation sessions, and my stints in solitary. Each time, Clara would ask me why exactly Abu Nabil had decided to make me a special case. As our conversation ended, we were joined by Baltazar. He told me that he had no intention of stopping there, promising books and materials so that we could keep ourselves busy. He jokingly apologized in advance, saying that although I was a committed Communist, he wouldn't be able to forward me the works of Marx and Engels. Later I learned that the only censorship was of books with a communist tone. I assured him that the most useful book for my Muslim friends would probably be the Koran. Before Balthazar and Clara left, I again stressed the lack of medical care and drugs. The guards seemed anxious when these visits were over. They questioned us endlessly, prodding us to tell them what we had told the ICRC. Abu Nabil was himself quite worried. He summoned the most malleable detainees to his office, hoping to invite their confidences.

Despite my fears, the visitors and the letters kept coming.

In December 1995, I saw my mother for the second time. There was more of a lightness between us; we even allowed ourselves a few jokes. When I told her that she hadn't changed a bit, she reassured me that they had kept her in the icebox since my arrest. She never told me about her own period of detention, here in this very same place. I found out later that before being arrested she had been given some good advice by my aunt, a veteran activist who had been imprisoned several times in the past, and who this time was only put under house arrest in our place in Deir Mimas. In total, I would see my mother six times within the walls of Khiam, the last in August of 1998.

That same month, the promises made by the ICRC began to take shape. The guards finally handed out books to read. This long hoped-for gift came on December 18. A week earlier, I had received a package containing my first book in eight years: the Bible, in an Arabic translation. My Muslim companions were presented with the Koran. From then on, we were given a regular supply of books that we had to return in exchange for new ones. Our "library" was quite diverse. It contained a large number of religious works, for Christian and Muslim women alike, but also books ranging from biographies (I remember one about Gorbachev) to scholarly works (like Dominique Chevallier's academic study of the history of Mount Lebanon), and even to romance novels written by Barbara Cartland that were quite out of place in the context of Khiam. It was even more surprising to read, in the introductions to some religious books, passages celebrating resistance against the occupation. There was even a historical novel set during the time of the British Mandate, a tale of one Jordanian man's resistance. It wrung tears from the eyes of its readers, each of whom compared the hero's story of political commitment with her own.

We also received textbooks for foreign-language instruction in French and English, but nothing that would familiarize us with a specific academic discipline. I set myself a strict limit when it came to reading: I would read no more than fifty pages a day, making sure I didn't damage my eyes after so many years without books. Of all the books in circulation, I particularly liked *Men and A Peace* by Carole Dagher, a Lebanese author. It was the story of the Israeli-Arab peace process launched after the Gulf War, culminating in the accords signed between the Israelis and the Palestinians. The book also described the effects on Lebanon and the Occupied Territories. It was a unique opportunity for me to learn what had been going on in my country and the region, during the years marked by the end of the civil war.

In 1996, the ICRC sent us materials—wool, cardboard, paper, paints, and beads. Even before this wonderful delivery, I had knitted little gloves for all the members of the ICRC: Badia, the translator, Baltazar, Clara, and all the rest. Each glove contained a small pocket, inside of which was a knitted flower. For me, to help meant to offer one's hand, and the flower protected inside the glove symbolized the human being. I had also knitted roses for Clara and for Corinne, another member of the ICRC. When the door of the cell I shared with two other detainees opened and the guards dropped a bag of materials inside, we couldn't believe our eyes. Haniya and Fatmé worked late into the night, making bracelets, earrings, and necklaces. I settled down to make a geometrical drawing, which I dedicated to the ICRC. Then we decided to organize ourselves into a workshop—I would draw while my friends painted.

We didn't know what to do with the cardboard, and it intrigued us. As a last resort, we decided to ask one of the guards, Samira, to find out what the men used it for. We were staggered by her response. Once again, we learned that they were evidently much more resourceful than we were—some of them even seemed like real artists. We were determined to find out more. To convince us, she smuggled over a few of their cardboard creations, and we couldn't help admitting their superiority. We copied their model for making prayer beads, and we were also inspired by their work in making greeting cards. Since many of the inmates were Shiites, they often drew the upraised hands of the famous Imam Ali holding his sword. Once we even dedicated a drawing to the secretary-general of Hezbollah, Hassan Nasrallah, featuring a play on words: *Al nasr nasr allah*, or "Victory is the victory of God." Our ploy didn't fool the guards, who confiscated the drawing straight away.

After all, we were still in prison.

15 HANAN

After my friend Kifah was released in 1994, I sank back into the daily reality of the camp.

Every moment was a fight against this world of incarceration and the rules it imposed on us. It was not a one-sided struggle—the prison walls had their faults and weaknesses. The more Abu Nabil strove to break the inmates' resistance and make them collaborate, the more we tried to make use of whatever connections, however distasteful, we could establish with the guards. With one of them, Joumana, I eventually developed a kind of complicity, even though of all the guards she was the harshest with the girls. She didn't much care for her colleagues, and hated the general climate of suspicion encouraged by Abu Nabil. She was the only one to risk bringing the male guards into the women's section of the prison, using all kinds of excuses to achieve this. Since she didn't have anyone else on hand, I became a kind of confidante. I was kept informed of all the internal workings of the camp, without even having to ask. Sometimes she even let me leave my cell at night, in secret, so that she could confide in me. I was delighted by this short spell of freedom stolen from Abu Nabil.

I also tried regularly to sow seeds of doubt among the women who had become collaborators. I told them that Abu Nabil's promise of freedom was often just a ruse, and that their situation was not so different from ours—as soon as the need arose to scrounge up some information, they, too, were thrown into solitary. After much convincing, some of them developed a kind of *modus vivendi*: they would offer only trifles to the interrogators, and would keep silent about our secret arrangements, large and small. And our ingenuity didn't let up for a moment.

The other women prisoners and I had worked out a new way of communicating, far more effective than our mailbox in the shower-room. We had managed to run a wire between adjoining cells by way of the cell windows. Once night had fallen, we could use it to pass messages along, or even little things like the cigarettes and matches so coveted by some of the detainees. We called our system the "elevator" or the "donkey." It bore witness to our strength of will, our ability to build a parallel life in Khiam. In my eyes, it was a continuation of the struggle we had fought outside of the prison.

In 1996, the arrival of another prisoner gave me new solace in this path. In Hanan, I discovered another militant friend. Kifah, my first comrade, was the repository of a history: the struggle of the Palestinians against the State of Israel. Hanan, for her part, shed light on another movement: the rise of Hezbollah in Lebanese society. Hezbollah, formerly a small radical group, was now firmly rooted in Lebanon's Shiite population. It had sworn to defeat the Israeli soldiers and their Lebanese mercenaries, and, increasingly, it had become their worst enemy.

Hanan had been arrested on a false pretext in 1996. The forces of the "security zone" had correctly identified her brother as a Hezbollah leader. By throwing her in Khiam, they hoped to gain some precious information about the workings of the armed group, whose military actions were growing more and more effective. On Hanan's arrival, she told us about Operation "Grapes of Wrath," launched by then Israeli Prime Minister Shimon Peres a few weeks before the 1996 Israeli elections. Lebanon was yet again subjected to a massive bombing campaign, the aim of which was to break Hezbollah. Yet the region's most powerful army was unable to dislodge the resistance fighters. They had melted into the Lebanese population, and from their bases they sent salvos of Katyusha rockets raining down on parts of northern Israel. We could hear the echoes of Israel's storm of fire from our cells in Khiam. It ended with a reverse effect after the massacre of Cana, when a site belonging to the United Nations Force for Southern Lebanon (FINUL), where hundreds of civilians had taken refuge, was bombed. The Naqura accord established an "April entente," putting an end to the crisis. The accord recognized the right to resist the occupation on the condition that civilians on both sides be spared.

When Hanan arrived in Khiam, I was the only female detainee. My companions had all been freed, benefiting from a favor that had been stubbornly refused me: the Israelis and Antoine Lahad had vetoed my release. Once in the prison, Hanan followed the usual "course": placement in isolation and sessions of interrogation and torture. Thanks to my contacts among the guards, I quickly found out who she was. I had heard her name before, and soon realized that she was a Hezbollah militant.

My first contact with her came when I caught her hanging at the window of the little cell, just as I had done a few months earlier. I gestured to her, signaling that she had better close the window as quick as she could to avoid the guards' reprisals. The young woman surprised me with her intelligence; in the blink of an eye, she had grasped the situation. A little later, I communicated with her by humming religious songs in a low voice.

From a distance, we sized each other up.

A trust began to develop between us. She quickly broke with our prisoners' instincts, not hesitating to take the maximum number of risks in getting messages to me when she was brought to an interrogation. Right away, I made her presence known to the ICRC team who had come to inspect the prison— her arrival had been hidden from them. At that moment, Khiam held only three women, compared to several dozen men.

Hanan soon made use of a technique for communication developed in the new cells built to give the ICRC visitors a better image of the prison. The sinks, an unimaginable luxury just a few weeks earlier, were connected by pipes that could be used to converse discreetly. You simply had to talk quietly over the drain, then bend your ear to listen. I passed along some elliptical messages hidden in seemingly innocuous songs, then told

her briefly of the traps that Khiam contained, sketching por-
traits of the interrogators with whom she was so brutally confronted.

These interrogators soon realized that the young woman
was not simply the close relative of a military chief. She was also
an active militant, who had been used as a courier. Hanan, for
her part, told them nothing. She responded sharply when they
truncated the name of Hezbollah secretary-general Hassan
Nasrallah, omitting the honorific title of *Sayyed*, or descendant
of the prophet. Of course, this threw them into fits of incredible rage.

Thanks to our conversations, Hanan managed to catch her
interrogators unawares. Once, I told her that one of them, who
was trying to pass himself off as a Christian with her, was actually a Muslim. A few weeks later, she left him speechless by
telling him, after faking some serious reflection, that he was
definitely from a Muslim village.

When a collaborator was placed in her cell, Hanan made
another brilliant move. The woman, trying to win Hanan's
trust, pretended that she, too, had been harshly interrogated.
But Hanan had been warned by my counsels. She quickly spotted traces of lipstick on the woman's mouth, and compliment-
ed her on the high quality of her beauty products. The collaborator, confused, swore that it was just her natural complexion.
Hanan didn't stop there. In minute detail, she questioned the
woman, who apparently made all sorts of errors in describing
places where she had supposedly spent many hours. Suddenly,
Hanan asked her to name the color of the latrine bucket used
in what she said was her cell. The woman, stunned, mumbled
the color fuchsia, to the great pleasure of my young Shiite
friend. She reminded the woman that the buckets were made
from olive oil jugs; she didn't know of any brands packaged in
such a rare color. A bit later, again following my advice, Hanan
set out to look for a possible bug hidden in her cell. After
searching meticulously for many hours, she did indeed find
one, and secretly stopped it from working.

Abu Nabil had already heard that one of Hanan's first acts

had been to lift the mirror in the interrogation room, checking to see if it hid some kind of listening device. He gave her full credit, telling her that such experience was unimaginable for someone of her tender age. In fact, Hanan was no beginner; she had been a militant since childhood, so to speak. She did, however, make a mistake with the head of Khiam by telling him her pseudonym in the resistance: Zahra. The name rang a bell with the security services. In their files, they found a set of plans stolen in Beirut outlining weapons transfers. The plans had been put together by a certain Zahra. It was Hanan, at the age of only fourteen.

For both of us, fate would soon begin to work in our favor. Through a combination of circumstances, Hanan was placed in my cell. For the first time in eight years, I shared, with some stability, the life of another prisoner. For six months, until January 1998, our hardships were the same.

By nature, we were quite different. Hanan was a headstrong young woman, never willing to compromise. Although naturally calm, she could easily be raised to anger. She was tall, with a melancholy disposition, and so beautiful that her natural grace was cause for jealously among the female guards. Unable to mask her feelings, she responded tit for tat when provoked by the interrogators, whatever the cost. She wore the veil, and was equally attached to her party and her faith. But this didn't stop her from being very open to other ideas and religious beliefs—she was never one to preach.

Although I was regarded as a Communist and a Christian, I had no trouble developing a deep friendship with this committed militant. For her, resistance to the Israeli occupiers was all that mattered. If she ever sensed the slightest uncertainty in my mind, she was quite capable of distancing herself from me. She was a woman of action, ready for anything under any circumstances, while I was more inclined to wait for the right moment and the appropriate means.

Still, we shared the same vision: a resistance movement in which each could find his or her own place fighting against an occupying army. One of my creations during this time was a picture that could be read as a number: 425. It was the number of the UN resolution adopted in 1978 calling on Israel to pull out of the occupied zone in Southern Lebanon. I was careful to make sure the number didn't jump out from the page. The slightest mention of the text, like any reference to the occupation of our land, was of course forbidden in Khiam.

Hanan and I spent our days talking politics, reading, and singing together. I introduced her to Marcel Khalifé's political verses, and she taught me the militant songs of Hezbollah. In the beginning, we were in relatively high spirits. When our families were authorized to visit, we often found ourselves side by side. The mutual introductions delighted us, although they irritated our guards to no end.

In turn, our parents asked us each to watch over the other; we definitely had the reputation of being excessively hotheaded.

After just a few weeks, Hanan fell sick, with an insidious and persistent pain in her stomach. The situation soon began to worry me. Khiam was unforgiving when it came to illness. My friend had begun to vomit blood. Her stomach infection couldn't be treated in such an unsanitary place and without qualified personnel. The prison administration had to be convinced to allow Hanan to go, under escort, to the hospital in Marjayoun. After a hard-fought struggle, we succeeded. With her hands bound and her head covered by a hood, she finally left the prison to undergo medical tests.

In the hospital, the results were inconclusive—no diagnosis could be established. This first visit would not be her last. The weeks passed, and my friend's worrisome condition meant more time in the hospital. To her family, Hanan denied everything, struggling to reassure her parents that she was in perfect health. For my part, I began to fear that the news would be bad. What if her sickness was a form of cancer?

As her visits to Marjayoun continued, I became stricken with fear. Her absence began to weigh on me. In fact, the hospital was not unfamiliar to me. Several years earlier, I had been briefly admitted because of dental problems; in the end, the doctor who operated on me had turned out to be quite incompetent. The security services were probably afraid that the prisoners might escape, so they were admitted one by one, and then chained to their beds during their stay. Even in the hospital, their twisted schemes continued. During one of Hanan's many stays, a man with a shaved head called to her from the window of her room, asking her if there was anything she needed. He became quite insistent. My friend didn't move a muscle. She guessed that it was probably a trap set by Abu Nabil, who hoped to justify his opposition to her long periods of hospitalization.

After many weeks of pain and fear, Hanan was finally released on the strength of her medical dossier. For the security services, she had become a burden; they balked at taking responsibility for the prisoner's ever-more frequent trips to and from Marjayoun. Again, I had lost a close companion, but at least I knew that she could finally hope to be well cared for.

The powers of Khiam had once again been thwarted.

16 FREEDOM

The ICRC, by bringing us mail and visitors, changed our lives.

I had seen my mother for the first time in eight years. Afterwards, our meetings became almost regular, although this still depended on the good graces of my jailers. During our second visit, in December 1995, we finally had the chance to hold and hug each other, but then for another five months this privilege was denied me. Abu Nabil was still after me, vicious as ever. In 1997, two more visits were set up. Once, my father managed to come, and I was reunited with him, too. He said as little as ever, which exasperated my mother. "Why come, if you're just going to sit there and not say anything?" she shot back at him with her usual spark. Then visits between prisoners and their families were cut off again for ten months.

After Kifah's release in 1994, the gates were periodically opened to let out more prisoners. Each time it was a celebration, even for those of us who had to stay. I was happy to see those detainees who had done nothing wrong regain their freedom. I knew why I had been thrown in here. For most of the women, locked up and forgotten for years within these grim walls, this was not the case; the security services had simply wanted to turn them into collaborators. The departure of my best friend also made me more optimistic. If she had managed to find her freedom, my turn would inevitably come. It was only a matter of time. The year 2000, that magical date, was still tucked somewhere in the back of my mind. There were still a great many male prisoners, and they still suffered extremely harsh conditions. But the ever-smaller number of women also helped change our daily routine; we were now permitted to take walks in the little courtyard adjoining our cells.

When it came to my release, my mother was more impatient than I was. Convinced that I was hiding something, she asked me about it every time she came to visit. I just answered that some time later I would be allowed to go.

In 1996, a wild rumor began to make the rounds of Beirut: I was to be released. My father tried to get information from the political authorities, who assured him that I was at the top of the list. Hezbollah said that it was working for my emancipation. Some journalists, and a few of my friends, even came to wait for me in Nabatiya, close to the occupied zone. My mother declined their invitation, but at home she worried her heart out, feverishly anticipating the news of my release. The presence of my friends came as a surprise to people in the South, and they quickly cleared up the misunderstanding. A release was indeed scheduled, but not for me. My mother, still in Beirut, was crestfallen.

Once more, we had to wait.

That same day, in fact, the cell door did swing open. The guard called one of my two cellmates. "Get your things," she said. "You're leaving." The young woman began to gather her belongings. The guard came back and called to the second young woman in my cell: "Pack a bag. You're going, too!" While the two detainees were getting ready, I wondered what would become of me. The minutes trickled by, but the guard did not return to make a final announcement. The two young women and I congratulated each other, and then they were gone. I was left alone, with the same hopes and the same passion to hold my own against Abu Nabil.

Because of my solitude and isolation in Khiam, I didn't quite realize that, throughout the Middle East and in France, special groups had been formed to work for my release. In Paris, a "Committee for the Liberation of Soha Bechara" had been created to spread awareness about Khiam; there was also a special committee of university professors. Immediately following my arrest, the Lebanese Communist Party had hired—without my knowledge—a French lawyer, Monique Picard-

Weyl, to defend me. She was full of energy and determination. She, in turn, got the Israeli lawyer Leah Tsemel to take up my case. Just as she had done for Kifah, Leah Tsemel fought a legal battle for me against her own state. For her, the stakes were simple: to prove that Israel sanctioned my detention in Khiam, and therefore to demand that my case be heard, with all due process, in an Israeli court. Slowly, her efforts began to bear fruit. She was soon able to prove that Antoine Lahad carried an Israeli passport. In France, where the SLA chief's family had moved after my operation, government officials were increasing their contacts with the Israelis on my behalf, but this shadow diplomacy was painfully slow. Still, French public opinion played its role: *Le Monde* printed a petition signed by many well-known figures. Even my mother, herself so removed from politics, went to Paris, then to Strasbourg, where she spoke at the European Parliament, and then to Quebec, on the invitation of Amnesty International.

In June of 1998, the sixteenth to be precise, the men's section began to bubble with an unusual excitement. They were getting ready for a huge release of prisoners. There was to be an exchange with the Israelis, who wanted to retrieve the remains of soldiers killed outside the occupied zone. We heard them read off a long list of family names, nearly fifty in all. There was banging on the cell doors, and voices cried out in answer. From our cells, we caught one name above all others: Mohammed. He had planned operations against the Israelis; if he was released, we were sure to follow. One of the women was particularly moved to hear his name: his wife Fatima, a prisoner in Khiam herself.

On the other side of the wall that separated us from the men, the final preparations for departure were being made. Still, no one had come to our side. Then all was quiet. For once, the women had been forgotten. Fatima, sure that her husband had been freed, simply laughed.

But our joy was short-lived. We soon realized that Mohammed had not been freed, but only transferred to another cell. To show that he was still there, he called to some inmates locked up nearby. I called out to Fatima in turn, trying to let Mohammed know that she was still here, too.

Another false alarm.

Summer went by, and in mid-August I was once again allowed to see my mother. To be reunited with her filled me with happiness. I returned to a kind of routine, which left me completely unprepared for the events of September 3rd. That morning, at 7:50 a.m., a guard, Alïa, came in. "Get your things!" she said. "What did you do to make Abu Nabil want to punish you and send you to cell number 1?" "Nothing," I answered distractedly. I was sure I was going to be released. The guard had said nothing, but I was sure of it. It was going to be today. There were only four girls left. The international campaign and the pressure from the lawyers had paid off: Israel had decided to wash its hands of such a difficult prisoner. My turn had come to leave the walls of Khiam behind. I gathered my belongings and changed cells. Once there, I showered and brushed my hair.

Then I waited.

They brought me to the SLA doctor, who inquired about my general health, and then filled out a brief report. He turned towards me once more, congratulated me, and handed me a few pills. "Take these before you go," he told me. "You haven't been in a car in a long time."

It was now 8:30.

The guards brought me into Abu Nabil's office. My old enemy, who seemed slightly on edge, sat behind his desk. A man was waiting beside him; I thought I recognized Abu Samir, the man who had escorted me to Israel just after my assassination attempt ten years earlier. He looked much older. Abu Nabil spoke. "You are to be released." He didn't add the slightest commentary. "This was in your bag when you arrived." I looked over at his desk and spotted my bag, a tube of sunscreen, and some perfume. The director of the prison questioned me: "Nothing missing?" On our arrival, our valuables had theoretically been put inside a safe. It must have swallowed up my watch, because as my fingertips brushed against the objects in my bag, I didn't feel it there. A few tapes of then-popular disco music were also missing, and—of course—my revolver. But these disappearances didn't shake the feeling of calm that had gradually come over me. Abu Nabil couldn't resist one last taunt. He mentioned the name of one of my friends who had already been released. "Did you know she married a man who was already married?" I didn't flinch. And so Abu Nabil handed me over to Abu Samir.

There were no parting words between us.

I went to cell number 1 to get my things and then I left. On the way out, I saw my two cellmates, Samira and Inntisar, perched at the window, their faces wet with tears. I knew, from having witnessed the release of many others, that their tears of pain were mixed with tears of joy.

We moved towards the gates of Khiam.

I had left the camp twice in ten years, both times to visit the hospital in Marjayoun. Then, I had gone hooded and handcuffed, seeing nothing of the prison or the journey. This time, though, I left with my head held high.

There were four of us in the car bringing me to freedom: the driver, Abu Samir, and a member of the security services who sat in back and watched. The car sped downward around the turns. I stared out the window, wide-eyed, remembering the little villages, the sharp bends in the road, noticing here and there some changes in the landscape. In no time, we were in Marjayoun.

I had a moment of doubt. What if I had not truly been released? What if I had been brought here simply to be confronted with Antoine Lahad? As we drew near the SLA chief's house, I prepared myself for this possibility. But the car did not turn off towards that fateful place. It kept on its way, finally stopping in front of Abu Samir's office.

We went inside.

The SLA official turned to me. "Do you know that your cousin Issam is dead?" he asked. I hadn't yet heard that he had, in fact, been killed in a car accident in France. I answered Abu

Samir with another question: "What is your name?" Taken
aback, he immediately responded, "Abu Samir." Then, slowly,
he passed me a form to sign. I read the first few lines. It was an
agreement not to commit any act that threatened the security
of the country, and to give them any information liable to be
used by the Lebanese Army. I read this a few times and then
skimmed over the whole document. There was no letterhead
on the form. It was anonymous. I smiled. "It's only a formality,"
explained Abu Samir, handing me a pen. With a shrug, I signed
the sheet of paper, asking him sarcastically if he needed me to
put my initials anywhere. The answer was no.

At that moment, Barbara from the ICRC came into the office.
Abu Samir officially handed me over to the International
Committee.

I was free.

Barbara embraced me. She told me that she had brought
some clothes, a sweater and a pair of pants, more presentable
than what I was wearing. I thanked her, but said I would stick
with what I had slipped on that morning: a pair of jeans, a light
shirt, and a belt that I had made with my own hands.

In the lot outside Abu Samir's office, a car marked ICRC was
waiting. We climbed in and set off for Beirut. The car took a
route unfamiliar to me. My eyes moved greedily over the coun-
tryside. We passed a few Israeli military units. Mechanically, I
filed away their unit numbers. The other passengers in the car
were carried away with joy. Paradoxically, I was calmer than
they were. Most likely the strange acceleration of history had-
n't hit me yet.

It was now 9:15 in the morning.

On the radio station *Voice of the People*, they announced my
release. Then, in Beirut, all the other stations interrupted their
programming to pass on the news. Journalists began to follow
the car, hoping in vain to catch my first reaction. But the ICRC
had given strict instructions: there were to be no interviews in
the occupied zone.

I knew that ten years had gone by since I last drove through
the occupied zone, but I couldn't trace the passage of time in

my surroundings. Barbara handed me a cellphone so that I could talk to my mother. Our conversation was happy and short. "Yes, I'm doing great. See you soon!" Barbara watched for my reaction to this magical new kind of phone, but I wasn't surprised—it was in line with stories told to me by new prisoners in Khiam. In the car, we put on some music. Barbara said that I probably wouldn't have heard these songs before. I told her that, thanks to the comings and goings of the detainees and to the guards' radio, I had heard all the new popular songs, too.

Our driver was wondering what the best route was to make it quickly to Serail, the seat of the government, where we were expected. He left the main road, turning onto an access road. When we arrived, I understood his concern. This time, the rumor mill had worked: there was a huge crowd gathered before the building. The ICRC car came to a stop. As I got out, I was greeted with cries of joy. At first a bit stunned, I recognized my father. He was waiting accompanied by the Prime Minister's bodyguards. As I went up the stairs to the Prime Minister's office, I recognized one face, then two, three, four faces. All my friends were there. Their features seemed unchanged, as if all those years had truly counted for nothing. Our hands fluttered, waved in greeting, almost touching, and then I went to rejoin my family, who waited for me in the lobby of the governmental palace.

During those first few hours of liberty, I felt like I had been swept into a whirlwind.

I was received by the Prime Minister, Rafic Hariri, and we posed for some photos. Then I gave a very long press conference. I was surrounded by Communist Party bigwigs, most of whom I didn't know: the current Secretary General, his predecessor, and many more. The Communists, who during my captivity had elected me to their National Council, stood all around me. I was not at all prepared for the new exercise of dealing with the media. I tried my best to draw their attention to the fate of those who were still imprisoned. Then the questions began to rain down. I was asked if I would be ready to do an operation again, and questioned at length about the torture administered in Khiam.

The assault of journalists didn't stop with the end of the press conference. I returned to our house under the eye of television cameras. The house had become a permanent media center, swarming with so many people that we started to fear our little balcony might collapse. At midnight, exhausted, I left for my uncle's to get some rest. The next morning, I woke up with a strange feeling—the opposite of how I had felt during my ten years in prison. Before opening my eyes each morning in Khiam, I had the impression of being at home in Beirut. For a long time in Beirut, I felt like I was waking up in prison.

The days that followed were filled with interviews and press conferences. I was never alone. My mother watched over me with jealous care. The Communist Party decided to provide me with a bodyguard; he stayed with us at our house, which annoyed me to no end. Of course, my mother was not exactly pleased by the Party's invasion of our personal life. After a few days, I took the bodyguard aside, tactfully assuring the man who was supposed to protect me that I had no need of his services.

As the weeks passed, I was never left in peace, never able to rediscover my life. My liberation had turned into a kind of national holiday. During the three months that followed September 3rd, thousands of visitors streamed into my house and the Party offices. They didn't let up for a moment. I was moved by their devotion to the values of the Resistance—at least, that's how I'd like to keep it in my memory.

At the time, I felt the weight of all those stolen years. I had been roughly shaken back to life, and I found it hard to find the rhythm of a peaceful existence. But somehow, I had to invent the next step, find another form of commitment. An idea began to take shape: a voluntary retreat far from Beirut, far from Lebanon, where I could get my bearings and find myself again. The French embassy in Beirut had told me, the very day I was released, that France would welcome me for as long as I liked. After thinking about it for a few weeks, I decided to accept. My mother was overjoyed. Every time I walked out the door in Beirut, she imagined that I was leaving for another mission in the occupied zone.

Earlier, I had been told that there was a message for me at the Communist Party offices. I knew immediately who had sent it. Rabih, my superior in the resistance. Picking up our old clandestine habits, we arranged to meet in secret. There, far from watchful eyes, we were reunited.

He had sent me into the lion's den. The place where I had burned to go. Every morning and every night, he had wondered about the fate of his young insurgent, caught in the trap of Khiam.

That day, we had almost no need for words.

EPILOGUE

Khiam was liberated on May 24, 2000, at the same time as the rest of South Lebanon, by bare-handed villagers. For years, they had been haunted by the tortured cries emanating from the camp. Now, columns of civilians made their way up towards the prison. They met with no resistance from the guards and the SLA militiamen, who had all decamped at midnight the previous night. The villagers butted up against the cell doors. They broke open the locks, bringing back to life haggard men and women who were dumbfounded by this sudden reversal of history.

In the first weeks after the fall of Khiam and of the occupied zone, Antoine Lahad, chief of the zone's military forces, took refuge in Tel Aviv. In France, the committees working for the release of Khiam's prisoners were ready for him to return to his apartment in Paris, where he had moved his family after my operation. They hoped to launch a suit accusing him of war crimes and crimes against humanity. Like him, most of the former guards of Khiam had also gone to Israel, where after the debacle they found themselves stranded in temporary camps. They were eager to get away, the sooner the better, to find a home somewhere that was more accommodating about their past. This was, of course, the case for Abu Nabil, along with most of the prison staff. Out of all the guards, only one, Alïa, decided to stay in Lebanon. When I returned to the South for the first time, no one knew what had become of her.

I visited Khiam and went back to my village of Deir Mimas, where I hadn't set foot since 1988, the year of the operation. Afterwards I divided my time between Lebanon, staying with my family, and Paris, where I studied Hebrew. I stayed in touch with Kifah. My dear friend had married a Lebanese man. She now lives in Beirut with her two children: a son, Ayman, and a daughter whom she named Soha after me. Palestinians in Lebanon are treated like second-class citizens, and like all of them, Kifah is not allowed to work. But she continues to struggle on behalf of those who were detained in Khiam, and those still held in Israel despite the IDF's retreat from the occupied zone. During my visit, I also saw Hanan; she and her husband are Hezbollah party activists. They have a little son, Abbas.

For my friends and I, there was life after Khiam. For a time, with the great joy of the liberation of the South, life even became beautiful. It was a rare moment of unity for the Lebanese. For fifteen years, with guns in hand, they had torn each other to shreds, and after a peace that refused to deal with the damage they had done each other, they remained deeply divided, too irresponsible to heal such painful wounds. The liberation showed how our civil war had been, like any fratricidal conflict, a vain illusion—when compared with the strength of our resistance against the Israeli occupation.

Khiam grudgingly returned to life so many damaged human beings, cracked and broken. Like all camps of its kind, its goal was to humiliate, to crush, to deny the existence of those it fed upon.

There are still dozens of Khiams around the world. Let us never forget them and finally tear down those walls, once and for all.

There remains the basic cause for which I fought: a free Lebanon, a country at peace, but one also grounded in the ideals of justice and democracy. This is above all a question of memory. If the people of Lebanon let themselves forget, then this hope will be lost and the spirit of the Resistance vanish.

I accepted the idea of dying for my country. I feel connected to the whole planet, to all of humanity, but Lebanon was where I was born and where I grew up. For me, the idea of my country is as simple as the air I breathe. I belong to this piece of earth, and it was from this piece of earth that they tried to banish me. I became a child of war. We never appreciate what it means to live in peace until that peace is no more. It must be understood what it is to grow up under an occupation, to live at the mercy of checkpoints and curfews, stripped of liberty and identity. At some point, with all the massacres, with all the killings, my own blood began to beat in rhythm with the blood around me. I decided to join the struggle. No amount of indoctrination can drive someone to act if that person does not believe in the cause, has not understood it, has not decided to live or even die for it. I knew what was in store, but this knowledge had no power to stop me. When I joined the Resistance, after four years of searching, I did not go alone. My family, my friends, my people—everything that made me who I am—all of it went with me. In the same way, I did not act in my own name as an isolated individual. I felt like all the Lebanese were at my side. My act, the operation itself, was a letter sent to them. In the face of the madness of civil war, it was a message of resistance directed against the real enemy.

In Khiam, I tried to keep resisting. It was the same struggle fought with different weapons, still against the same occupying power. Now the struggle became constant, a matter of holding your own at every moment. Those who broke down, or became informers, were those who did not understand the reality of occupation and resistance, those who could not grasp the radicality of freedom. Once in prison, they reverted to their own basic patterns of behavior, falling back on illusions or a sense of guilt. For me, the fact that I was a girl, that I put my family in danger, that I was incarcerated—none of this mattered. To have stopped fighting would have been to turn my back on what it means, for all of us, to be human.

Every day, every minute, you hold yourself together—you try not to end up in that other prison, horrible and definitive, the mental hospital. You hear voices of men screaming, of women pleading, you see a mother whose son is torn from her, a grandmother dragged into the torture room, you try to tell the girl in the next cell not to scratch the eczema that devours her body

You don't give in, you don't give away any emotion, or the enemy has won. The prison locks you inside your thoughts, time washes away your memories, your loves, your childhood. Fear is always there. You know that in yourself you have found your ultimate adversary, and that you must once again go beyond yourself to find your freedom, once more, you must resist.

Sometimes in the camp, a laugh, a little improvised scene was enough to overcome the horror. Today, some innocuous thing can take me back for a moment to my solitary cell with its floor of beaten earth. But only for a moment. It is not this memory which fills me now, but that of a whole people and its future—the spirit of resistance. Because what I did, I did for tomorrow's children, for that fragile time when they will play in the shade of trees, and the air will echo with their shouts of joy.

Printed in the United States
by Baker & Taylor Publisher Services